# *Contents*

# THE COSMIC CHRIST

## *Paul Writing To The Colossians*

## Martin Connolly

Second edition September 2023

Published by

Oakleaf Publishing

Front Cover Image:

This is an adjusted photographic reproduction of a two-dimensional, public domain work of art by El Greco (1541–1614) St Paul

# Preface to the Second Edition

Having continued further study into the wonderful book of Colossians, I decided that there needed to be further clarification of some topics and a fuller expansion of the Jewish thinking behind Paul's writing.

It is the hope that this will give further insights into what Paul was teaching the Colossians and through that understand more of how this can be brought into the lives of Christians today.

As a Pastor, it is always good to ensure that fresh food is supplied to the flock and it is my continual prayer that through these pages, the flock will indeed be fed and encouraged.

For clarity in understanding the Jewish and Christian texts, The Jewish texts will be referred to by the name known to Paul and Jesus, the *Tanach* and the Christian texts will be referred to as the Early Church Texts.

Pastor Martin Connolly

Sept 2023

# Introduction

In the very beginning, in the mystery that was before human consciousness, there was God. As was revealed to Moses, out of that mystery, a Voice spoke and brought into existence the great cosmos (Col 1:16-17). This Word that was spoken was the Messiah (Christ), the anointed promised one who would become flesh and dwell with humanity (John 1:1-3). Here the Jewish Messiah was the centre of the cosmos, the all-powerful God in flesh (Col 3:9). However, the time would come when man would turn away from God and seek answers to the great wonder of the cosmos, through worship of the natural things observed. The sun, moon, trees and rivers would be looked to, for answers to the mysteries of life and to explain tragedies and triumphs.

Abraham would abandon these idols and usher in, through his descendant Jacob/Israel, the chosen people who were charged with carrying the truth and hope of the Messiah. But their journey would be on a path that would touch foreign religions that would attempt to contaminate the truth and draw God's people away from truth.

Their captivity in Babylon would particularly cause such influences, that needed Nehemiah and Ezra to purge the nation on the return to their homeland (Ezra 6:21, Ezra 9:1-15). The Jewish nation would be then be dominated by the Greeks and Romans, both of whom would bring the influence of their foreign gods and beliefs among the Jews. The Pharisees and others such as the Essenes would strive to keep the religion pure, often through extremes. The event of the birth of Jesus would once again bring a cataclysmic change as the Messiah is revealed in Him. For Paul, he would declare the resurrection of Jesus as the great confirmation of Jesus as the Saviour and Messiah;

> *"Paul, a servant of Jesus Christ, called to be an Apostle, separated unto the gospel of God, which he promised beforehand through his prophets in the holy scriptures, concerning his Son, who was born of the seed of David according to the flesh, who was declared to be the Son of God with power, according to the spirit of holiness, by the resurrection from the dead; even Jesus the Messiah our Lord" Romans 1:1-4*

The diaspora, which had scattered the Jewish people among the nations, especially exposed God's people to foreign beliefs, including the growth of angel worship and syncretism of beliefs. This was particularly true of the Greco-Roman peoples who quite readily absorbed the gods of conquered nations into their pantheon of gods.

We now turn to Colossae which was a city in the Lycus Valley in Asia, close to Ephesus and Laodicea. It was a centre of trading near the great trade route that passed through that area. Once a great city of the region, with a famous wool industry, by the time of Paul, it had been reduced by the Romans to 'village' status. Within it the diversity of religions had taken root. It was probably during Paul's visiting nearby

Ephesus that Epaphras (Col 1:7) (and Timothy? Col 1:1) were inspired to take the Gospel to Colossae and found a company of God's people.

Greek asceticism and angel worship were well established at Colossae, with a popular legend of the archangel Michael being implored to aid the church at a time of disaster. Michael is supposed to have split a rock to swallow a stream of water sent to destroy the church. This led to the cult of Michael being established. It would appear that a heresy which fused Greco – Roman myth, eastern religion, Judaism and Christianity had become aggressive in Colossae. This was a false gospel that was being preached, not the later Gnosticism that has often been thought, but a mixture as mentioned above. It is this that causes Paul to write.

Paul's letter is a remarkably short letter, to explain the Messiah as head of the Church and to guide the saved from a drift into heresy. It is to declare the greatness of Jesus the Messiah as the centre of the cosmos and the Truth made flesh releasing man from the tyranny of false religion.

The study is not designed as a review of the debates over authorship etc. These are covered elsewhere and have no merit in what is designed as a study to encourage and build up saints in their devotion to Jesus the Messiah. It is a study from a Pastor's heart, seeking to preach the glorious truth of the Cosmic Christ. The earliest church fathers were clear that the Apostle Paul wrote the letter and this study accepts that view. The letter was a 'prison' letter probably written shortly before 60

AD as Paul does not mention the earthquake of that year that devastated the region and destroyed Colossae. Most likely, it was written from Rome. It is the most Christ centred book of the Scriptures, in that it speaks of His pre-eminence, and the greatness of His work.

In covering how the believer has been given freedom in Jesus the Messiah, the letter also gives guidance as to practice of faith in the Messiah in daily life. In that, the letter is of great encouragement as it speaks as fresh today as it did in that early days of the community of Jesus.

# Chapter One

*Colossians 1:1*

*"Paul, an Apostle of Jesus Christ by the will of God, and Timothy our brother,"*

The things to note in the introduction begin with the use of his name, Paul. Unlike our letter writing where the name comes at the end, in this culture the name came first. This was especially true in letters of authority. In using it here, where Paul will go on to speak against heresy, he is making clear the authority to write to the recipients. He goes on to emphasise this with using his title of Apostle. Paul did this often in his letters, as he was the object of ridicule and undermining by some others. (See Gal 1:11-12; 1 Cor 9:1-6; 2 Cor 11:22-33; 2 Cor 12:1-12) Furthermore, Paul makes clear that he is an Apostle not by the will of men, but by that of God Himself. This has important implications for the believers to seek to know God's will for themselves. This is not arrogance or the abandonment of humble submission to others, but a sincere desire to serve God according to the grace God gives for that which He calls. Paul wrote:

> *"For through the grace given to me I say to everyone among you not to think more highly of*

*himself than he ought to think; but to think so as to have sound judgment, as God has allotted to each a measure of faith." (Romans 12:3)*

This ability to acknowledge what God had done and to maintain the humility in that calling was a hallmark of Paul. (See Rom 15:15; 1 Cor 3:10; Eph 3:2; Eph 3:7-8) We also note that Timothy is mentioned alongside Paul. Paul does not include Timothy in the calling of Apostle, clearly showing that each one is called differently. Timothy would be aware of the letter and from other places happily accepted his role of Paul's companion and 'son'. Again, we learn to be humble in accepting what God has called us to, without jealousy towards others *seen* to be called in a 'higher' way. Each one of the saints of God must accept the power of the Spirit in their lives and discover for themselves the call of God to service - then, as Paul, to single-mindedly get on with that call. In this it is not for the saint to envy another's mission, but to look to one's own calling and to do that with all one's strength, in the power of the Holy Spirit.

Paul often mentioned companions especially when there was a need to give authority to them or to link the recipients with Paul through the person. Here Timothy was from that region and would be known to them. Timothy was 'our brother' and they too were Paul's brothers, united by the Messiah. Such is the family of God in Jesus, all related by brotherhood. This is the truth of true relationship with Jesus – where it truly exists in the heart of a child of God, he or she is at one with God's children, whatever their background or race - Jews and Gentiles truly one new man in Christ. (Eph 2:15) This relationship is the experience of true believers, wherever they meet, being joined in that unity that comes through Jesus.

*Colossians 1:2*
*"To the saints and faithful brethren in the Messiah who are at Colossae: Grace to you and peace from God our Father."*

Although most translations render the verse as above, there are in fact two groups being addressed in the Greek. The saints elsewhere and faithful brothers and sisters at Colossa. The elsewhere is probably the nearby Laodicea, where the letter is to be also read (Col 4:16). Paul here describes the believers as saints - holy ones, thereby making clear how being in the Messiah Jesus transforms the individual from the un-holy to the holy. As will be developed in this letter, the un-holy are made holy through the work of the Messiah. In this then that all the holy ones are called to faithfulness in their relationship to Him and to each other as brethren. It is into such holy unity we are called.

Furthermore, Paul extends two vital blessings that are found in Christ – grace and peace. We could rush past this greeting and miss their importance. Firstly grace. Paul has in mind the Hebrew word *chen* or *chesed*. The use of these words focus is on the giver and means that the giver, who is greater, has had compassion on a lesser. In that compassion, love, long-suffering and mercy is shown. This is fitting, as we understand being in Jesus. In this we are being shown mercy through grace that has pitied our helpless estate and in compassion has lifted us out of the mire. That it is all the work of God, is a constant theme with Paul as seen in Ephesians:

> *"For by grace you have been saved through*
> *faith; and that not of yourselves, it is the gift of*
> *God;" (Eph 2:8)*

Secondly the blessing of 'peace' also would be *'shalom'* in Paul's mind. This goes beyond the simple desire of 'peace' for a person but extends to wanting the best for their welfare, in every aspect of their being. The usage is also beyond the traditional greeting, in that Paul will have to address controversy. His desire for their true *shalom* is such that he will not shirk from declaring the truth (See also Eph 6:20, 1 Thes 2:2). This has implications for Christians who compromise 'for the sake of peace and unity'. If we desire the best for others we will not shrink back but declare the truth in all grace, so that their *shalom* will be full. In this Paul again would in other places (1 Cor 10:11, Eph 6:4, Titus 3:10) use the term *'noutheteō'* to convey the idea of admonishing with love, the errors of believers. The Jewish Paul no doubt has in mind, *mûsâr,* the Hebrew correcting of error and straying from doctrine of the Lord. This is seen in many places, note it here in Job:

> *"Behold, blessed is the man whom God*
> *corrects: Therefore despise not thou the*
> *chastening (mûsâr) of the Almighty" Job 5:17*

Paul in his writing to the Colossians wants them to be blessed as they stay faithful to the Lord Jesus. He also makes clear that this grace and peace is not from men, but from God who is also our Father. This greeting is a true blessing and should be encouraged to be the conversation of all those in Jesus, to their brethren.

### Colossians 1:3
**"We give thanks to God, the Father of our Lord Jesus Christ, praying always for you,"**

Paul and Timothy are included in the giving of thanks for this community. Often Paul would express thanks for those he wrote to, even when he had difficulties with them or had to bring chastisement. (See Rom 1:8; 1 Cor 1:4; Phil 1:3; 2Ti 1:3; Phil 1:4)

Such an attitude would guard Paul's heart as he carried out the Lord's work. How often do we have wrong attitudes towards others because the heart is not thankful to God for what has been done in Christ for us? As we hold that attitude of thankfulness then so our views of others will be filled with grace. Paul unites the Father and The Son in unity as the object of his prayer – the Son through whom all access to the Father is gained. As Paul is to refer to the heresy that is threatening Colossae, he is also stating the threefold title of the Son, as Master, Saviour and Messiah. We see also that Paul's prayers for them are not infrequent but he prays 'always' for them. Let us too be spurred on to love and good deeds in this area as we make it our regular practice to pray for those who we are connected to in fellowship.

**Colossians 1:4**
**"since we heard of your faith in Christ Jesus**
**and the love which you have for all the saints;"**

The writer of proverbs was inspired to write:

*"a good name (shem) is to be more desired*
*than great wealth, favour is better than silver*
*and gold." (Proverbs 22:1)*

The Hebrew word *shem* used in Proverbs and no doubt the Hebraic idea is in Paul's mind, is not just a label of identity but far more. It is the character and inner being, attitudes etc. of the person – their reputation. The recipients of Paul's letter had a good name, a good reputation, in that they were known for their faith in Christ Jesus. Note it was not for their intellectual prowess or wealth materially, not even the size of their congregation, what matters, as Paul would write elsewhere, it is

*'...faith working through love'. (Galatians 5:6)*

6

This knowledge had come from Epaphras their founding minister. He had seen this community threatened by heresy and the temptations to run after other things. Yet they had remained steadfast and loyal to Jesus. Trusting Him for all they needed to run the race of faith. Not only this but their reputation for loving one another. This was the mark that they truly belonged to Jesus. (John 13:35) This was the evidence of their salvation. John wrote:

> *"We know that we have passed out of death into*
> *life, because we love the brethren. He who does*
> *not love abides in death." (1 John 3:14)*

When a community truly loves, then there is life in that community, because they are connected to the head Jesus Christ by their faith. Faith without love is an empty profession that cannot be truly of Jesus. Faith and love, of and in, Jesus, together make the powerful witness to the living Saviour, and it is for that, Paul can commend this community. That every community of Jesus should have such a name and reputation would be the greatest witness to the Gospel of our Saviour.

**Colossians 1:5**
**"because of the hope laid up for you in heaven,**
**of which you previously heard in the word of**
**truth, the gospel"**

Here is the third element of the three qualities Paul would often refer to – hope. Here the tense means that it was some past action that continues into the present. Their faith and love had arisen out of this hope - a hope, born out of the action of Jesus the Messiah, whilst also including something future, is something very real to give encouragement today. This hope was not a vague thought that something might happen, but a rock-solid outcome of faith. More than this, the Christian hope is itself the Lord Jesus. Paul wrote:

*"an Apostle of Christ Jesus according to the commandment of God our Saviour, and of Christ Jesus, who is our hope," (1 Timothy 1:1)*

It is faith in, and of, Him that gives eternal fellowship with Christ, it is 'laid up' or better, according to the language, 'reserved' for saints. Because of this security the Colossians could have faith, love and hope that enabled them to live out their Christian walk. This hope is described in Hebrews:

*"This hope we have as an anchor of the soul, a hope both sure and steadfast and one which enters within the veil," (Hebrews 6:19)*

Once man was cut off from God, without hope but now Jesus had come and died, was buried and rose again, and had removed the curtain, so that our hope is an anchor for the soul. No longer were the saints to be tossed about on an emotional troubled sea, concerned for the future.

Now they had a hope that enabled them to have continuing faith and love that would hold them fast until the return of Jesus. This hope, the Lord Jesus Christ, had been preached to them and it was the word of truth – the Good News. Paul wrote:

> *"For this reason, I also suffer these things, but I am not ashamed; for I know whom I have believed and I am convinced that He is able to guard what I have entrusted to Him until that day." (2 Timothy 1:12)*

This is what is at the heart of the Gospel – Jesus Christ who is our hope – He is the end of man's needs. In Him all things are fulfilled. The word of truth sets men and women free from the slavery of sin and death. It gives them the confidence of an eternal future with Jesus. This hope enables the Christian to look on the world with reality. The difficulties and threats around need to be faced: not with fear but with hope. Hope that does not disappoint, (Rom 5:5) but which recognises the sovereign nature of the One in whom they hope. The Colossians had this but it was not just for them.

**Colossians 1:6**
**"which has come to you, just as in all the world also it is constantly bearing fruit and increasing, even as it has been doing in you also**

*since the day you heard of it and understood the*
*grace of God in truth;"*


Not only was this word of truth – the Gospel - for the Colossians - but it was also at work in the entire known world. The message of Christ had been released from a small Middle Eastern country and was now spreading across the earth, just as Christ had said:

> *"but you will receive power when the Holy*
> *Spirit has come upon you; and you shall be My*
> *witnesses both in Jerusalem, and in all Judea*
> *and Samaria, and even to the remotest part of the*
> *earth." (Acts 1:8)*

Paul also had in his heart his own commission as an Apostle. He also had been called, as he had written earlier, to bring this Gospel to the Gentiles. This is the work of the Holy Spirit, who takes the sparks, from the burning flame of persecution in Jerusalem, and scatters them over the entire world. (Acts 8:1) Paul is also contrasting the heresy that was trying to gain a foothold in Colossae. This heresy would be fleeting and fruitless. It would produce unrighteousness in its practice and would be death. It would be for a secret elite. But where the Gospel of truth is preached, it is for everyone. With it there is righteousness and peace. It brought life and hope. This was indeed the evidence among the believers at Colossae. Since they had heard the Gospel and understood its message, such fruit had been produced among them.

The message they had heard and understood was 'the grace of God in truth'. This is the message all believers are to grasp. The world and its entire people lay under the sentence of condemnation and death. God, who would be justified in sending all men to eternal separation, had acted in His Son and made a way for all to know life. As it is written:

> "The Lord is not slow about His promise, as
> some count slowness, but is patient toward you,
> not wishing for any to perish but for all to come
> to repentance." (2 Peter 3:9)

The grace of God is seen in its magnificence when we consider Jesus the Christ, who in order to open the way to God and life, died when man was alienated from God. His death was the merit for all men, who had no merit - His resurrection the merit of life for all who deserved death. This is the grace of God in truth. It is this great understanding that brings fruitfulness to lives. The false religion at Colossae for the few stood in stark contrast to this message of life for all that is the Gospel.

> **Colossians 1:7**
> **"just as you learned it from Epaphras, our beloved fellow bond-servant, who is a faithful servant of Christ on our behalf,"**

Epaphras had brought this message of truth to them. Note they had 'learned' it. The sense of the language is that they had increased in the knowledge of these things by practising them. Epaphras, like any preacher, had delivered the truth, but it could not bear fruit in anyone who would not take it to heart and live it out. Such was the parable of Jesus in the Sower. (Matthew 13) The believer is called to be a disciple – a learner – who grows in the knowledge of God. All Bible Study or listening to preaching, is a pointless exercise of knowledge for knowledge sake, unless it is followed by application, that is true learning. Paul also makes mention of Epaphras, who is with him in prison. (Phil 23) He is spoken off with great affection in that he is 'beloved'. Such is to be the tender feeling between those who labour for Christ. They are locked in a loving covenant with God, and the bond that holds all in that covenant is love. This is the testimony of belonging to Jesus.

Furthermore, Epaphras is a 'fellow bond-servant'. The use of this term by Paul is important. There is an acknowledgement that there is equality between the great Apostle and this man – equal in service differing in calling. The term used is pointing to them both being simply servants of a greater Master. They have been bought; hence they are bonded – to each other and to the Master, the Lord Jesus. The price of their purchase is spoken of by Paul elsewhere, the blood of Christ. (1 Cor 6:20, 1 Cor 7:23) This is the truth for all believers. We are all equally servants of Christ, each with different giftings and callings. Each one is to seek God for the field of their own labour and then to get on with their service, as was said earlier. In this service we work together as the Body of Christ for the greater glory of God – fellow bondservants.

In this service as with Epaphras here, we are to be faithful. This is not simply a matter of speaking of faith in Christ but being trustworthy – worthy of trust. This is what God looks for in His servant children. In their service they grow as friends of God. Friends who can be trusted to do what He asks of them. Note too that Paul makes clear that Epaphras is a 'servant of Christ'. Albeit here, we see, it is on behalf of Paul and his companions that Epaphras is serving. This is to be our attitude in all things, to serve as unto God in Christ. Later in this letter (Col 3) Paul will clarify this to teach that the work we do for men, we do heartily as for the Lord.

### Colossians 1:8
**"and he also informed us of your love in the Spirit."**

Epaphras had not only brought to Paul the knowledge of what was the dangers threatening the church at Colossae, but he also informs Paul of the many positive things in the church. Here the report is of the love, also expressed in verse 4. The love was *agapé*, that love which was of God Himself. It is worthwhile here referring to an aspect of the Colossian heresy that Paul will speak of later. The religious climate in the Greek world was very different from the Hebrew mindset about God that Paul had. The Greek's had a very different view of love. The Greeks word *eros* was rooted in sexuality but developed into an ecstatic worship of gods, where reason was left behind. This worship would include temple prostitutes and relations between humans would be loose and promiscuous. The Greeks also had a word for relationships between a human, which was based on emotion and that were non-sexual, *phileō*, and this was reserved to social relationships. The Hebrews had one main term that covered the love between God and man and man and God. The same word would be used of relationships between humans, were it was seen as devoid of any selfishness, as it was to reflect God's love. Whilst it was not devoid of emotion, it was a determined decision, an act of the will. In the Septuagint (LXX), the word *agapé* was mainly so used.

Paul's use was important in terms of trying to get to the heart of intimacy in our relationship with God, that was deep, but of course absent of any sexual connotation. It was a love that was a willed choice that would be applied to God and to fellow believers. That is why the letter speaks of *'love in the Spirit'*. This *agapé* love is a love that is inspired off, and in, the Holy Spirit. The Spirit always points us to Jesus Christ. So, *love in the Spirit*, is a pure love that seeks the best for the other, and is reflected in Christ's love to us, in His choice to lay down His life for us, whilst we were still sinners (Rom 5:8). We are to love others in that same manner as God loves us. This was not just the thought of Paul but of the Spirit who inspires the same urging in other places.

14

*"And he answering said, "You shall love the Lord*
*your God with all your heart, and with all your soul,*
*and with all your strength, and with all your mind; and*
*your neighbour as yourself"* (Luke 10:27)

This was the reply of a lawyer who questioned Jesus, *"Teacher, what shall I do to inherit eternal life?"* Jesus in turn responded with a question as to what the Law said. The lawyer's response was the Jewish *shema*:

This was on Paul's mind: the eternal salvation of those at Colossae. The love of God had sought them and saved them and they should maintain that pure love of God towards their Saviour and to each other. There should be no mixing of the immoral practices of the heretics with their Godly love.

This is a mark of those who belong to Christ that they have this *agapé* love for each other:

*"By this all men will know that you are My*
*disciples, if you have love for one another."*
*(John 13:35)*

Those at Colossae could be seen to be of the Messiah because of their *'love in the Spirit'* – a pure undefiled *agape*.

**Colossians 1:9**
**"For this reason, also, since the day we heard**
**of it, we have not ceased to pray for you and to**

**ask that you may be filled with the knowledge
of His will in all spiritual wisdom and
understanding,"**

Isn't it interesting to see what moves Paul to prayer? *'For this
reason,'* Paul writes. The reports of Epaphras to Paul about the
Colossians were of danger from heresy, but also of faith, hope and love
as being evident within the community. Since the day Paul had heard of
these things about them, as the text means, he is moved to pray for them.

What follows in the next few verses is that prayer, started here in the
first petition. Again, it is good to note what Paul prays. His request is
that they might be *'filled'*. This word is to remove any vacuum in the
spirituality of the Colossians. There must be no room left for heresy and
wrong thinking. They are to be filled with *'επίγνωσιν τοῦ θελήματος'* –
'knowledge of His will'. This Greek phrase was used at that time as a
code for followers of Christ. The knowledge of God's will is not an
intellectual exercise but the awareness of a relationship with God
through the One who expressed the will of God perfectly - Jesus Christ.

*"Jesus said to them, "My food is to do the will
of Him who sent Me and to accomplish His
work." (John 4:34)*

This is what we need to pray for one another in that we would also
be filled with such knowledge. How this comes about is through the
gifts of the Holy Spirit. The Spirit's gifts of wisdom and understanding

are not like fleshly wisdom and understanding. The wisdom of the world is foolishness.

> *"For the wisdom of this world is foolishness*
> *with God. For it is written,* He that taketh the
> wise in their craftiness: " *(1 Corinthians 3:19)*

The *gnosis* (knowledge) of the Colossian heresy was foolishness and so Paul is praying for the true wisdom of the Spirit for them. This wisdom is linked to *'understanding'* as translated here. The root Greek word is from 'two rivers meeting'. The notion is based on the idea of two (or more) things coming together bring perception, insight or revelation. This insight was a revelation from the Spirit into the things of God. This was for all God's children and not an elite few that the heresy might suggest.

Paul is praying powerfully for God to equip his readers, and indeed us, to be filled with such knowledge of God's will, with wisdom and revelation so that we might live for Him.

> **Colossians 1:10**
> **"so that you will walk in a manner worthy of**
> **the Lord, to please Him in all respects, bearing**
> **fruit in every good work and increasing in the**
> **knowledge of God;"**

Paul continues to point out that the result of what he has written in the previous verse has consequences; firstly, that they should 'walk'. The use here by Paul is echoing his Jewish understandings. The Hebrew word *halakah* that is probably on Paul's mind, means 'to walk'. It is also the word used to describe the way that the people of God should live out their daily lives. For Paul this must be in a manner 'worthy of the Lord'. Some other texts have 'worthy of God'. However, it is likely that it is Jesus that Paul is speaking of. The child of God bears the name of Jesus. How he behaves in the world will either bring honour or disgrace to the name of Jesus. Paul wrote to the Thessalonians:

*"so that the name of our Lord Jesus will be glorified in you, and you in Him, according to the grace of our God and the Lord Jesus Christ."*
*(2 Thessalonians 1:12)*

This is why it is important to examine our manner of walking or how we live. Does it glorify the Lord?

If flows from this that we are to seek 'to please Him (the Lord) in all respects'. Again, it is to the Thessalonians that Paul writes:

*"Finally then, brethren, we request and exhort you in the Lord Jesus, that as you received from us instruction as to how you ought to walk and please God (just as you actually do walk), that you excel still more." (1 Thessalonians 4:1)*

There then follows a list of instructions for living out the Christian life. Note Paul also urges the Thessalonians, who are living or walking well, to excel still more. Paul is saying to the Colossians and the Thessalonians, never to become complacent but to stay alert. In this they will please God. This follows on from his commending their faith. Faith and pleasing God are intimately connected. It is written in Hebrews:

> *"And without faith it is impossible to please Him, for he who comes to God must believe that He is and that He is a rewarder of those who seek Him." (Hebrews 11:6)*

Paul is making clear that the Christian life is a life of faith that seeks to live in a manner that ever pleases the Creator and our Father. This life can only be lived out in Christ by the power of the Spirit.

It is this same Spirit who is at work in believers to produce fruit in every good work. The Gospel is clear that good works cannot save, but they are the outworking of faith. As Paul wrote to the Ephesians:

> *"For we are His workmanship, created in Christ Jesus for good works, which God prepared beforehand so that we would walk in them." (Ephesians 2:10)*

This 'bearing of fruit' expression reflects Paul's use in verse 6. Just as the fruit of the Gospel was increasing, so too it was expected the fruit of faith would increase and would bring the knowledge of grace to the world.

The text needs attention here in the last phrase of the verse. The increasing is not 'in' the knowledge of God but 'through' or 'by' the knowledge of God. What that means is that the fruit should be increasing as their knowledge of God increases. The more we come to understand the Good News and the work and person of Jesus Christ, the more we will know how to please God and seek to do the work He has set us to do. Again, Paul is making a comparison between the heresies that saw secret knowledge as a key to spirituality and maturity and the knowledge of God, which was the true basis of any maturity in spiritual matters.

*Colossians 1:11*

*"strengthened with all power, according to His glorious might, for the attaining of all steadfastness and patience;( joyously)"*

The 'joyously' at the end of the verse fits better with verse 12 and will be discussed there. (The division of chapters and verses were an insertion of the 13th and 16th century not in the original Scriptures.) But as Paul continues his prayer, he uses the Greek tense to show that the strengthening is ongoing. The believer lives out the calling of Christ in a dangerous and deceitful world. To not only endure but also to press on in the life of Christ we need to be strengthened daily. It is because the Colossians were under such pressure from heresy and false teaching that they particularly are the object of Paul's prayer to strengthen them.

The power of this strengthening was not from human effort or resources but was according to *'His (God's) glorious might'*. In the Greek it reads *'the power of His glory'*. The whole glory of God was the power that would strengthen the believers at Colossae. Such is the inheritance of the saints. Jesus promised that the believers would receive power from above (Acts 1:8) When the Holy Spirit came. That same Holy Spirit is the necessity of every believer. This is why Jesus urged His followers to ask the Father for the Holy Spirit (Luke 11:13). Without the Spirit of Christ, the believer can do nothing. (John 15:5 - The Holy Spirit is the *allos* (John 14:16) – the exact same as Jesus, and when Jesus says we can do nothing apart from Him, He is referring to the believer's need of the Spirit of Christ to do anything.

It is of interest that the inspired word of Paul here speaks of the power for the purpose of steadfastness and patience. Many would seek first to think of the Spirit's power for miracle or signs, but Paul is a wise Pastor. He is acutely aware that the pressures on Christians will mean that their faith will need to hold. Miracles and signs, as so often seen in Scripture, would not cause people to endure in faith. There needs to be a deeper sense of steadfastness in the innermost being. It is to be a faith that is not linked to trends and experience but is rooted in a Spirit filled heart that will trust the Lord in all circumstances. Paul has already commended the Colossians for their love, faith and encouraged them in hope. Now he prays for the strengthening of power for steadfastness and patience, as the writer to the Hebrews wrote:

> *"And we desire that each one of you show the same diligence so as to realize the full assurance of hope until the end, so that you will not be sluggish, but imitators of those who through faith and patience inherit the promises" (Hebrews 6:11-12)*

It was Jesus, their hope, who had guaranteed the promises to those who would endure. Paul is also concerned that they run the race well and finish the course – and it is to this his prayer focussed.

*Colossians 1:12*

*"(Joyously) giving thanks to the Father, who has qualified us to share in the inheritance of the saints in Light."*

This verse is very awkward in the Greek. Some translations bring the word 'joyously' in this verse as it is better linked to the idea of thanksgiving. Our thanksgiving to the Father is to be with joy. Just as Paul had earlier addressed his prayers to the Father thanking Him for the Colossians, (Col 1:3) he now encourages them to be thankful with joy. This is to be the disposition of the believer, who as Paul goes on to say has been given a unique privilege. That privilege, is that the Father has 'qualified' them to share in the inheritance of the saints in the Kingdom of Light. That is that the Father has made them 'sufficient' or 'fit' for the Kingdom, as He has made all saints. Later Paul will again comment on the inheritance (Col 3:24) but as we turn to Peter we find his expansion:

> "Blessed be the God and Father of our Lord
> Jesus Christ, who according to His great mercy
> has caused us to be born again to a living hope
> through the resurrection of Jesus Christ from the
> dead, to obtain an inheritance which is
> imperishable and undefiled and will not fade

away, reserved in heaven for you," (1 Peter 1:3-
4)

In similar language Peter speaks of the mercy and hope of the believer who has an heritance reserved, or as Paul, 'laid up', for them. This inheritance is the act of the Father, who through Jesus, who was crucified, buried and raised from the dead, so that the believer could be so qualified. This is the cause for rejoicing. The believers could not achieve this in their own strength, but through faith, they had been brought to the Father. He had brought them to Himself. In considering Jesus and His suffering, they were to rejoice in this, as it was this selfless act of Christ that had brought them such benefit.

Furthermore, they had been brought into the Kingdom of Light, as Paul will continue to explain. This Light was Jesus, as prefigured at the beginning of creation, who had brought about these things. Paul will later record a hymn of praise to Jesus the Creator, who had made possible the re-birth of the believer.

*Colossians 1:13*
*"For He rescued us from the domain of darkness, and transferred us to the kingdom of His Beloved Son,"*

This idea of joy floods Paul and moves him to a peon of praise. Paul is acutely aware of his previous condition - a condition in which he needed to be 'rescued' or 'delivered' from. This is reflecting the helplessness that Paul had come to realise was his condition outside of Christ. He writes to the Romans:

> *"For while we were still helpless, at the*
> *right time Christ died for the ungodly."*
> *(Romans 5:6)*

Paul came to see that all his understanding about religion and being in relationship with God, had been built on wrong assumptions. His situation was as all men and is made clear by Luke:

> *"Because of the tender mercy of our God,*
> *whereby the sunrise from on high shall visit*
> *us, To shine upon them that sit in darkness*
> *and the shadow of death; To guide our feet*
> *into the way of peace. " (Luke 1:78-79)*

The Sun of Righteousness had risen with healing in His wings (Mal 4:2) on Paul and all believers, such as those in Colossae. In the helpless estate, men are living under the shadow of sin and its wages of death. It is a kingdom of darkness with error, deception, misery and spiritual death that brings separation from God. Paul rejoices because he has been rescued from this kingdom – this *'domain of darkness'*, as the text reads.

It is important to note the use of words by Paul here. In using εξουσία (*exousia*), Paul is speaking of 'authority' over someone. In the kingdom of darkness, the authority over the individual is all-powerful and makes the individual incapable of escape - helpless. Someone from outside the situation, of greater authority, must intervene and help the individual. This is the Work of the Father in Christ. Paul's mission and that of each believer is to declare the truth and freedom in the Gospel. The words of Jesus in Matthew are referring to this declaration:

> *"I also say to you that you are Peter, and upon this rock I will build My church; and the gates of Hades will not overpower it."*
> *(Matthew 16:18)*

When we read of 'gates' in Hebrew thought, we are reading about the authority of magistrates and elders who sat in the gates of cities. The faith in, and of, the Messiah that Peter had expressed was the bedrock from which the authority of the Kingdom of Christ would be exercised. The authority of darkness over men had been broken and the greater authority of Christ now reigned. God had now given helpless man the means of deliverance or rescue from this domain of darkness.

When faith in Jesus Christ is exercised a miracle happens. There is a spiritual movement of the individual. He moves from the authority of the kingdom of darkness and is translated or transferred to the Kingdom of the Son, He (The Father) loves, as the Greek reads. It is not the Kingdom of realised glory, that we are moved to, that comes at the end when Christ returns. The Kingdom of the Beloved Son is the Kingdom that is now present and is to be advanced by the preaching of the Gospel.

This is the role of Church, of all believers, to declare the wisdom of God to the principalities of darkness that their rule is finished. Paul writes in Ephesians:

> *"so that the manifold wisdom of God might now be made known through the church to the rulers and the authorities in the heavenly places." (Ephesians 3:10)*

Praise as a weapon in this warfare is proclaimed by Peter:

> *"But you are a chosen race, a royal priesthood, a holy nation, a people for his own possession, that you may proclaim the excellencies of him who called you out of darkness into his marvellous light. " (1 Peter 2:9)*

It is in this spirit Paul continues his hymn of praise.

### Colossians 1:14
**"in whom we have redemption, the forgiveness of sins."**

We read here the means of our deliverance. It is redemption. A ransom has been paid. It is in Ephesians Paul expands this thought:

> *"In Him we have redemption through His blood, the forgiveness of our trespasses,*

*according to the riches of His grace."*
*(Ephesians 1:7)*

It is the blood of Christ that has paid the ransom – the price of our forgiveness from sin. It has sometimes been a mistaken understanding that the ransom was paid to Satan. This is not the case. Neither was the ransom paid to the Father, His love of the Son would never require it. The ransom is the price paid to justice. The act of Adam to disobey God meant that the sentence of death must be carried out according to the demands of justice and righteousness. The demand of justice must be met in order for the death sentence to be remitted from men. Someone must pay the price demanded by justice. That price is pure innocent blood. Why blood? The Scriptures state that 'the life is in the blood'.

*"For the life of the flesh is in the blood,*
*and I have given it to you on the altar to make*
*atonement for your souls; for it is the blood*
*by reason of the life that makes atonement."*
*(Leviticus 17:11)*

Only a perfectly pure life uncontaminated by sin must be offered to satisfy the demands of justice. That is why Peter preached:

*"And there is salvation in no one else; for*
*there is no other name under heaven that has*
*been given among men by which we must be*
*saved." (Acts 4:12)*

As commented earlier, the word 'name' in Hebrew thought is '*shem*', meaning the total nature, character and person. Only the nature, character and person of Christ was pure and holy enough to be the acceptable sacrifice to satisfy justice. In Christ is all justice satisfied and all who come into Him are in the wonderful position described by Paul:

> *"There is now no condemnation for those*
> *who are in Christ Jesus." (Romans 8:1)*

This is the great source of joy, that the redemption is for the forgiveness of sin past, present and future, and we are now no longer required to satisfy the demands of justice for our transgressions; something we could never have done anyway. In Romans Paul writes of Jesus:

> *"whom God displayed publicly as a*
> *propitiation in His blood through faith This*
> *was to demonstrate His righteousness,*
> *because in the forbearance of God He passed*
> *over the sins previously committed; for the*
> *demonstration, I say, of His righteousness at*
> *the present time, so that He would be just and*
> *the justifier of the one who has faith in*
> *Jesus." (Romans 3:25-26)*

As Peter also sums it up:

> *"For Christ also died for sins once for all,*
> *the just for the unjust, so that He might bring*

*us to God, having been put to death in the*
*flesh, but made alive in the spirit;" (1 Peter*
*3:18)*

Because the perfect sacrifice has been made to satisfy the ransom required by the demands of justice, all who come to faith in the work of Christ are forgiven their sins, on the merit of the ransom paid – the blood of Christ.

And so we see the reasons for Paul's great hymn of praise to Christ, one in which every believer is called to join!

**Colossians 1:15**
**"He is the image of the invisible God, the firstborn of all creation."**

This is an amazing beginning to Paul's great hymn. It is a statement of the nature of the cosmological Christ. In declaring Him to be the 'image', Paul is stating the revelation he has had on the Damascus road. No longer was his perception of Jesus after the flesh. As Paul wrote:

*"... even though we have known Christ according*
*to the flesh, yet now we know Him in this way no*
*longer." (2 Corinthians 5:16)*

Once Paul sought to destroy the followers of Jesus. He saw Jesus only as another man of many who had made false claims to be the Messiah. But on the road the divine Light with the *Bat Kol*, a voice from heaven, revealed Jesus as the true Messiah who had been raised from the dead. More than this Paul now had realised the truth as understood and taught by John:

> *"No one has seen God at any time; the only begotten God who is in the bosom of the Father, He has explained Him." (John 1:18)*

and as confirmed by Jesus Himself;

> *"Jesus said to him, "Have I been so long with you, and yet you have not come to know Me, Philip? He who has seen Me has seen the Father; how can you say, 'Show us the Father'?" (John 14:9)*

This word 'image' as used by Paul is to describe that Jesus is the imprint of the Father, as would be the image on a coin. If one wanted to know what the Father – the invisible God - was like, one had to look at Jesus. All that Jesus was and did, explained God and His heart for mankind.

In describing Jesus as the 'first-born' of all creation, we must not jump to the heresy that Jesus was a 'creation' or 'product' external to God. - a creation, as all other created things. Paul is speaking in earthly terms to convey the reality of Jesus as the pre-eminent revelation of God, who stands at the head of the family of God.

The term 'first born' is a Hebraic term of pre-eminence. In every family the first-born son was seen as the head in all things to the father.

In the father's absence, the first-born acted in his stead. In terms of the nations, God declared Israel as such:

*"Then you shall say to Pharaoh, 'Thus says the LORD,*
*"Israel is My son, My firstborn" (Exodus 4:22).*

Israel was to be the first of the nations and be a light to all the other nations (Isaiah 42:6, 49:6, 60:3). In terms of Jesus, He is the glory of the Father:

*"............... the glory of Christ, who is the image of*
*God." (2 Corinthians 4:4)*

For Paul declares:

*"which He brought about in Christ, when He raised*
*Him from the dead and seated Him at His right hand in*
*the heavenly places, far above all rule and authority and*
*power and dominion, and every name that is named, not*
*only in this age but also in the one to come. And He put*
*all things in subjection under His feet and gave Him as*
*head over all things to the church, which is His body,*
*the fullness of Him who fills all in all." (Ephesians 1:20-*
*23 NASB)*

In this Paul understands first-born to be of a royal family where Christ is the highest of Kings. In the family of God Christ is the first-born of other brethren:

*"For those whom He foreknew, He also*
*predestined to become conformed to the image of His*

*Son, so that He would be the firstborn [Pre-eminent]*
*among many brethren;" (Romans 8:29)*

In the 'Royal Priesthood' of God, Christ has first place and this Paul
will state clearly in verse 18. The writer to the Hebrews echoes this idea
of Paul, inspired by the Spirit:

*"And He is the radiance of His glory and the exact*
*representation of His nature, and upholds all things by*
*the word of His Power When He had made purification*
*of sins, He sat down at the right hand of the Majesty on*
*high," (Hebrews 1:3)*

In this pre-eminence Paul now sees the Creator role of the cosmic
Christ.

**Colossians 1:16**
**"For by Him all things were created, both in the**
**heavens and on earth, visible and invisible,**
**whether thrones or dominions or rulers or**
**authorities - all things have been created**
**through Him and for Him."**

Here Paul is as of John:

*"All things came into being through Him, and apart
from Him nothing came into being that has come into
being." (John 1:3)*

That Christ is the image of the invisible God, and is God, is seen in
this statement that Christ is the Creator. We cannot divide the Godhead
into separate beings, they are the revelations of the One True God. In
their oneness, when one acts, all act.

The imagery of Jesus as the King in Majesty, co-equal with God as
described earlier is expanded here. For Paul, Christ is the Light that
came forth from God at creation; His pre-existence and divine claims
now justified by His rising from the dead. The encounter with the
eternal Light of Christ had opened Paul's eyes to the astounding
revelation of his Saviour as the author of all things.

In creation, all things were the work of Christ, not a process of
evolution. There is no 'chance' in the invisible and visible order. The
creation is to a plan and purpose of God. To assume that Genesis is
some pre-historic myth conjured up by ignorant men trying to explain
that which they did not understand, is defeated here. In the sophisticated
Hellenistic world of Colossae, where philosophy and ideas were ever
present and where heretical teachings were trying to break in, Paul
makes clear that God in Christ created all things.

In using the ideas of 'thrones or dominions or rulers or authorities',
Paul is stating that kings and rulers on earth exist by Him and all the

powers of heaven in terms of angelic beings were also created by Him - they are all subject to Him. Furthermore, they were created by Him and for Him. In this all creation is to serve Him. When they rebelled, as did angels and as did Adam, they placed themselves in opposition to the plans and purposes of God. The same Christ will judge all things, as Paul declared:

> *"because He has fixed a day in which He will judge*
> *the world in righteousness through a Man whom He has*
> *appointed, having furnished proof to all men by raising*
> *Him from the dead." (Acts 17:31)*

That is why all men are called by the Gospel to bow the knee to Christ as Lord and Saviour now. As Paul also wrote:

> *"that if you confess with your mouth Jesus*
> *as Lord, and believe in your heart that God*
> *raised Him from the dead, you will be*
> *saved;" (Romans 10:9)*

To reject Jesus in life is to bring oneself under judgement. John writes:

> *"He who believes in Him is not judged; he*
> *who does not believe has been judged*
> *already, because he has not believed in the*
> *name of the only begotten Son of God."*
> *(John 3:18)*

The prophet Isaiah is inspired to record:

*"Turn to Me and be saved, all the ends of the earth; For I am God, and there is no other. I have sworn by Myself, the word has gone forth from My mouth in righteousness and will not turn back, That to Me every knee will bow, every tongue will swear allegiance." (Isaiah 45:22-2)*

Paul picks up this theme in writing to the Philippians:

*"so that at the name of Jesus every knee should bow, in heaven and on earth and under the earth, "*
*(Philippians 2:10)*

Paul's statement here in Colossians 1:16 is the source of joy to believers that the Lord Jesus Christ is sovereign. However, to those who reject Him, it is a warning to come to Jesus now and honour Him as Lord of all.

### Colossians 1:17
### *"He is before all things, and in Him all things hold together."*

Paul, having established the divinity of Christ, moves to continue his wonder at the power of Christ. He declares that Christ is before all things. The word has the clear indication that Jesus existed, before the whole of creation. This is confirmation of the Divine nature of Jesus the Messiah. Again, Paul is confirming John's message:

> *"In the beginning was the Word, and the Word*
> *was with God, and the Word was God." (John 1:1)*

The JW's will not translate this phrase according to the Greek, making the Word (Jesus) to be 'a god'. But we must resist their interpretation as the Greek reads, 'καὶ θεὸς ἦν ὁ λόγος'. This reads literally, 'and God was the Word'. It cannot be construed in any other way. There is no definite article before the word 'God'. In John's Gospel, we are seeing the Apostle, make clear that Jesus was with God, but to underline that Jesus was co-equal with the Father the Spirit inspires him to write in clarification, that Jesus was also God – *Yahweh*. Paul in Colossians here is underlining in his hymn of praise this same truth. This is no more than what Jesus Himself said when addressing the Pharisees;

> *"Jesus said to them, "Truly, truly, I say to you,*
> *before Abraham was born, I am."" (John 8:58)*

John the Baptist's own testimony also confirms that Jesus
was divine:

> *"John testified about Him and cried out, saying,*
> *"This was He of whom I said, 'He who comes after*
> *me has a higher rank than I, for He existed before*
> *me.'" (John 1:15)*

Even though John was older in age than Jesus, his claim is not to this existence but to Christ's eternal nature. And so Paul is proclaiming in ecstatic praise the deity of Jesus the Messiah and more than this, he exclaims the wonder of His power. This power of Jesus is that which is sustaining all things. The meaning is clear - the Spirit is reminding us that the power of the cosmic Christ is awesome. Consider what power is necessary to sustain the sun and planets? What power is necessary to ensure the ongoing movements of the universe, which even science admits, that one tiniest deviation from their course would bring chaos that is unimaginable. Heb. 1:3 also declares His greatness;

*"And He is the radiance of His glory and the exact representation of His nature, and upholds all things by the word of His Power When He had made purification of sins, He sat down at the right hand of the Majesty on high," (Hebrews 1:3)*

Isaiah wrote:

*"Who has performed and accomplished it, calling forth the generations from the beginning? 'I, the LORD, am the first, and with the last I am He.'" (Isaiah 41:4)*

Jesus Himself also declared:

*"I am the Alpha and the Omega, the first and
the last, the beginning and the end." (Revelation
22:13)*

When He decides to end all things, only then they will end. This is
the security of the believer. With so many voices declaring the end of
things with climate change etc., as if in some way man has control. God
has given him responsibility for the earth, not control. Paul's hymn
reminds us who really is in charge; Jesus the cosmic Christ. Paul's
rejoicing is not in his circumstances but in the view of Jesus he has in
his sight. Let us be similarly encouraged!

**Colossians 1:18**

**"He is also head of the body, the church; and
He is the beginning, the firstborn from the
dead, so that He Himself will come to have first
place in everything."**

Paul moves from the proclamation of Christ as head of the cosmos,
to be clearer about the body of believers. The heretical pre-Gnostic
ideas about how man related to the universe were in Paul's mind. Christ
is the head of the body of believers and also the body. (Eph 1:22-23)
He is the head, the pre-eminent one, of the redeemed community. This
further insight must have also come from Paul's Damascus road

experience (See comment on verse 15). Paul had been persecuting a heretical sect as he believed, until he hears the voice from heaven:

*"and he [Paul] fell to the ground and heard*
*a voice saying to him, "Saul, Saul, why are you*
*persecuting Me?" And he said, "Who are You,*
*Lord?" And He said, "I am Jesus whom you are*
*persecuting," (Acts 9:4-5)*

Paul now understood the reality of the mystical body of Christ. Those who have been redeemed from death through the work of Christ are moved from being part of the first Adam, to become the community of the second Adam - Jesus Christ - they are 'in Christ'. As He was living and was raised from the dead first (In terms that He would never die again, as had Lazarus for example.), then all who believed in Him would follow. Paul looked to that glorious day when as he wrote also:

*"so that He may establish your hearts without*
*blame in holiness before our God and Father at*
*the coming of our Lord Jesus with all His*
*saints." (1 Thessalonians 3:13)*

This pre-eminence of Jesus over all things is emphasized here. Paul believed in that great day, when in Christ's revelation at the end of all things, all would realise who Christ was and every knee would bow and every tongue confess Him to be the Lord of all things. Such then Paul continues to rejoice in this truth as we too are encouraged to do.

*Colossians 1:19*

*"For it was the Father's good pleasure for all*
*the fullness to dwell in Him,"*

That this speaks of the unity of the Godhead, in that there is pleasure in the Father's heart that the fullness of Deity is also in Jesus. Indeed, Paul writes also:

> *"[Jesus] who, although He existed in the form*
> *of God, did not regard equality with God a thing*
> *to be grasped," (Philippians 2:6)*

As the father had pleasure in Jesus and no rivalry was in the Father's heart, neither was it in the heart of Jesus. The hymn addresses the unity and love of the Godhead that must be seen in the Body of Christ, wherein which the fullness of God dwells, by the Holy Spirit. (Eph 2:22) Furthermore, Paul is also making clear that the heretical belief that the fullness of God could dwell in other things, such as nature, is false. Man can only find the fullness of God in Christ: any New Age belief or cult expression that would place God's fullness anywhere else is to be rejected.

*Colossians 1:20*

*"and through Him to reconcile all things to*
*Himself, having made peace through the blood*

*of His cross; through Him, I say, whether things on earth or things in heaven."*

In this last verse of the hymn, Paul carries on to write, that the Father's pleasure is also involved in the reconciliation. Isaiah writes similarly:

> *"But the LORD was pleased to crush Him, putting Him to grief; if He would render Himself as a guilt offering, He will see His offspring, He will prolong His days, and the good pleasure of the LORD will prosper in His hand." (Isaiah 53:10)*

That this offspring is the community of Christ, we find in Hebrews:

> *"For it was fitting for Him, for whom are all things, and through whom are all things, in bringing many sons to glory, to perfect the author of their salvation through sufferings."*
> *(Hebrews 2:10)*

The Father has through Christ reconciled all those who express faith in Christ to Himself. This work was achieved through 'the blood of His cross'. As discussed above in verse 14, the precious blood of Christ was the ransom that brought God's peace to men - this blood that satisfied justice and turned God's wrath away. What joy and what blessedness that concludes Paul's hymn. Before leaving this verse, it must be said that some, such as Origen, would use this verse to preach universalism of salvation for all men, all angels and even the Satan. This has become a modern belief in some places. This cannot be true as confirmed elsewhere in the Early Church Texts, (Matt 22:14 and the preceding parable illustrates this. Also, Matt 7:21)

*Colossians 1:21-23*
*"And although you were formerly alienated and hostile in mind, engaged in evil deeds, yet He has now reconciled you in His fleshly body through death, in order to present you before Him holy and blameless and beyond reproach- - if indeed you continue in the faith firmly established and steadfast, and not moved away from the hope of the gospel that you have heard, which was proclaimed in all creation under heaven, and of which I, Paul, was made a minister."*

Having first focused on Jesus and made Him magnified in the eyes of the readers – grace that allows truth to break through – Paul reminds them of their condition outside Christ. They were enemies of God, as he also told his Roman readers. (Rom 5:10) Such are all men outside of

Christ. Their hostility originated in the corruption of their mind by sin. Hence Paul writes in Romans 12:2:

> *"And do not be conformed to this world, but*
> *be transformed by the renewing of your mind,*
> *so that you may prove what the will of God is,*
> *that which is good and acceptable and*
> *perfect." (Romans 12:2)*

Because the world has ideas and principles that are foreign to God, they will lead to the evil deeds that should be left behind. The heresy trying to take hold among them was of the world and was hostile to Christ. They must realize that they can have no part of it, because they had now been reconciled through the very body of Jesus. Again, this is a possible reference to the heresy that would try to suggest Christ never suffered in actuality. That denied his being human as well as divine.

Christ had come as God in flesh and had partaken of man's nature, yet without sin. In His physical suffering and death, He bore the sin of man. This would enable man to be able to be justified before a holy God. Now they were *'holy and blameless and beyond reproach'*. The tense is both present and future. For those now in Christ, they stand justified, separated to God, and without any blame. This is the present state of all believers before God, because of Christ. Yes of course there is still a work to do in each believer, but that work is carried out, not in condemnation, but in grace. Indeed, as we are reminded:

*"For I am confident of this very thing, that He who began a good work in you will perfect it until the day of Christ Jesus." Phil 1:6*

This is our confidence in Christ Jesus. But not only this, Paul also confirms that the believer is *'beyond reproach'*. This is to make clear that there is no one who can bring accusation against the believer who trusts in Christ. Paul will later address the issue of the Colossians not judging each other in the matter of keeping religious rules (Col 2:16) because of the substance of what Christ has done. The heresy was bringing in various arguments and one may have been about how Jews and Gentiles should live in the light of Christ. Paul is giving assurance that there is no reproach in Christ.

Satan, who is the accuser of the brethren, has no claim and cannot accuse the brethren. In Zec 3:1-6 we see an amazing typology of this truth. The Theophany, the pre-existent Messiah, defends Joshua, as He defends all who trust in Him. This is the joy of the believer that he stands un-condemned and free because of Jesus!

Paul warns his readers to continue in faith in Christ as taught by Paul. They were not to be swayed by the heresy that was being preached. Their focus must remain on Jesus. Their faith was to be firmly established – well rooted. Paul will take this up again later in chapter 2 and is here preparing the ground. The believers must continue in faith through being rooted in Christ. They must maintain their feeding on Christ, in His word and not waver in belief.

Returning to his theme of hope, Paul urges the Colossians not to move away from this hope. The inference being that any hope offered by any other teaching is a false hope that will disappoint. They had heard the Gospel, the Good News of the work of Christ. The great hymn Paul has just presented demonstrated the exaltation of Jesus as the most powerful and pre-eminent of all. He was the only one who could guarantee the salvation of their souls.

This Gospel was even now, and would continue to be, preached everywhere. All men would be given opportunity to respond. Paul himself makes clear that was his mission. This was his calling and indeed the calling of all who profess Jesus as Lord and Saviour. The application for believers is to hold Christ before their eyes. He is the Messiah, who is the pre-eminent and supreme head of all things and especially of His Body, the Church. This same Christ through His death and the shedding of His blood has reconciled sinners to a holy God. This is the believer's joy and cause of great praise to our great Christ – Jesus the Lord!

> *Colossians 1:24*
> *"Now I rejoice in my sufferings for your sake,*
> *and in my flesh, I do my share on behalf of His*
> *body, which is the church, in filling up what is*
> *lacking in Christ's afflictions."*

Firstly, we see the attitude of Paul to his service for Christ. To bring the Gospel to the Gentiles Paul had suffered much and was now in prison. A look at 2 Cor. 11:23-28 will bring home the tribulations of Paul. Paul would not shy away from these sufferings seeing in them the identification with the sufferings of Jesus so that he could also share in the resurrection glory. As he wrote to the Philippians:

> *"that I may know Him and the power of His*
> *resurrection and the fellowship of His sufferings,*
> *being conformed to His death; in order that I*
> *may attain to the resurrection from the dead."*
> *(Philippians 3:10-11)*

Paul knew he was not alone in the evangelizing of the world he had other partners. (Phil 4:3; Col. 4:11; Phil 1:24) However Paul makes clear he is doing his share on 'behalf of the body'. This is the inspiration to us all to follow Paul's example and to be able to say that we are doing our share in the furtherance of the Gospel.

The next phrase has proved a difficulty in interpretation and has been used wrongly by some to suggest that Christians in their suffering can in some way make up for a deficiency in Christ's suffering. It led to a belief that self-inflicted suffering was to be a practice for the devout. This is a total misunderstanding of the language. Firstly, the word 'suffering' in Greek used here by Paul is never used in association with the atoning suffering of Christ. Secondly, other Scripture must interpret any individual Scripture and the overwhelming view is that the work of

Christ was complete. Paul's own hymn here in Colossians is a testament to the supremacy and completeness of Christ's work. Indeed, the Saviour Himself cried out, "It is finished!" (John 19:30) Hebrews 4 also makes clear that Christ rested from His work having done all that was necessary. The best commentators' interpretations are that the Body of Christ will endure suffering before the end. Paul lived in the shadow of the return of Christ and at his time there was a belief that the Body of Christ would go through a specified period and quantity of suffering.

Themes found in other Scripture suggest this to be so. (Matt 24:6ff; Mark 13:8; Luke 21:9; Rev. 6:10-11) Each member of the Body would have a share in that suffering and Paul was rejoicing that he has been able to contribute his share. Throughout the ages many have followed Paul's example and suffered for the Gospel and the blood of many Martyrs testifies to those who have done their share in the spreading of the Gospel of Christ. Let us take from this a prompt to remember in our prayers all those who even today, are suffering and dying for the sake of Christ and His body.

> *Colossians 1:25*
> *"Of this church I was made a minister according to the stewardship from God bestowed on me for your benefit, so that I might fully carry out the preaching of the word of God,"*

Here Paul is recalling verse 23, where he acknowledges his call of God. The word Paul uses is *'diakonos'* which normally is used for a Deacon, but the great Apostle is demonstrating his humble approach to his work for the body of Christ. He is a simple servant, called by God. In Paul's mind, in the following words he uses, Paul is addressing his Gentile audience and recalling how he became a minister of the Gospel to the Gentiles. We read of this in Acts:

> *"But the Lord said to him [Ananias], "Go, for*
> *he is a chosen instrument of Mine, to bear My*
> *name before the Gentiles and kings and the sons*
> *of Israel; for I will show him how much he must*
> *suffer for My name's sake.""* *(Acts 9:15-16)*

In recalling how he had suffered, Paul remembers the day Ananias spoke to him and told him of his Gentile mission. He was a chosen steward over this mission. It was for their benefit he had been called to this work of the Gospel in which he suffered. His passion for the work is seen again in the words he uses. He wants to see the Gospel fully preached. He wants all peoples and all places visited by this Gospel. His urgency is infectious, his passion admirable and calls to us to emulate him in this great mission; to see the Gospel of Christ proclaimed to everyone.

*Colossians 1:26*

*"that is, the mystery which has been hidden from the past ages and generations, but has now been manifested to His saints,"*

This verse is beginning to address again the heresy affecting the Colossians. The pre-Gnostic belief in the role of angels, and the need of secret initiations was an abomination that Paul will address later in Col. 2:18. For now though, Paul is making plain that a 'mystery' is now revealed. That it is being addressed, not only to humans, but to the demonic angels who are ultimately behind heresy, is made clear in another place where demons and magic was rife:

> *"and to bring to light what is the administration of the mystery which for ages has been hidden in God who created all things;*
>
> *so that the manifold wisdom of God might now be made known through the church to the rulers and the authorities in the heavenly places." (Ephesians 3:9-10)*

The Gospel is not only a proclamation to the world that is seen, but also to the unseen world, that Jesus the Messiah has won the victory over all demonic power. The means of salvation and deliverance was no longer a mystery but has now been revealed to all men – The Lord Jesus Christ! He and His salvation have now been revealed to those who are called to be saints, the holy ones of God. The Spirit quickens them and they respond in faith, and upon repentance are delivered from the domain of darkness. This is the great truth that the powers of darkness want to keep from the perishing. The Church's mission is to ensure that this does not happen as all are called to proclaim the Gospel.

But there is more to the mystery that would be in Paul's mind. This Pharisaic Rabbi would have believed that there was a 'chosen people' – the Jews. They were the only ones who held the truth about God. Entrance into this was only through circumcision and the keeping of the *Torah*. Gentiles may have a place in the world to come if they kept the Noahide Laws – a set of principles laid down by God through Noah. However, the Gentiles would always be inferior and certainly could never share in any meaningful way with Jews. To the Jew, the Gentile was no more than a dog. (See the incident with Jesus and the Gentile woman in Matthew 7). It is important to note that this attitude to Gentiles was localised to the area of Israel, particularly Jerusalem and was not universal. In the earliest centuries of the Diaspora, Jews and Gentiles often got along quite well. Room was often given to arrangements to allow some coming together of Jews and Gentiles, but there was even then a clear distinction made. For Paul the greatest revelation was in relation to the Messiah. He wrote:

> *"It was because of a revelation that I went up;*
> *and I submitted to them the gospel which I*
> *preach among the Gentiles" (Galatians 2:2a)*

As a Jew, Paul would have expected a Messianic figure who would have come as King of Israel to defeat the Gentile enemies of His people. He would set up the kingdom of Israel as first of the nations, wherein under His rule the Jewish nation would reign supreme. The idea that Gentiles could enter the world to come was accepted under strict conditions, but that Gentiles could have any part in the Messiah was unthinkable. This was the shocking revelation that Paul had – Gentiles could be saved through Jesus the Messiah by faith! He writes in a similar way to the Ephesians, as here to the Colossians, but with greater detail. It is worth reading in full:

> *"For this reason, I, Paul, the prisoner of Christ Jesus for the sake of you Gentiles-- if indeed you have heard of the stewardship of God's grace which was given to me for you; that by revelation there was made known to me the mystery, as I wrote before in brief. By referring to this, when you read you can understand my insight into the mystery of Christ, which in other generations was not made known to the sons of men, as it has now been revealed to His holy Apostles and prophets in the Spirit;* **to be specific, that the Gentiles are fellow heirs and fellow members of the body, and fellow partakers of the promise in Christ Jesus**

*through the gospel, of which I was made a minister, according to the gift of God's grace which was given to me according to the working of His power. To me, the very least of all saints, this grace was given, to preach to the Gentiles the unfathomable riches of Christ, and to bring to light what is the administration of the mystery which for ages has been hidden in God who created all things; so that the manifold wisdom of God might now be made known through the church to the rulers and the authorities in the heavenly places. This was in accordance with the eternal purpose, which He carried out in Christ Jesus our Lord, in whom we have boldness and confident access through faith in Him." [Author's emphasis] (Ephesians 3:1-12)*

Here is the amazing revelation. The Jewish body (community) was no longer to be simply Jewish; Gentiles could now become part of this body, through the body of the Lord Jesus the *Messiah*. This was no human revelation, but it was from the Spirit of God Himself. It was also not an Early Church doctrine but was already revealed to Apostles and prophets in the Tanach. Indeed, Paul expands this in Romans (and Galatians), showing Both Abraham – A Gentile - and David - a Jew - are equally saved by faith (Romans 4). This revelation is now manifested to all who would see. The early Church was no more than the Jewish community to whom the revelation came and was accepted. The mission of Paul particularly, expanded this to embrace the Gentiles who eventually became the largest population of the Church. Paul could write:

> *"There is neither Jew nor Greek, there is neither slave nor free man, there is neither male nor female; for you are all one in the Messiah Jesus." (Galatians 3:28)*

The thing to note is that this did not stop men being men, and women being women, nor Jews being Jews and Gentiles being Gentiles. It was simply the distinctions in these groupings, were irrelevant in terms of the equality of salvation. We who believe in Jesus are now all saints together by faith! Hallelujah! It is important to note that Paul was not seeking to teach that the belief in Jesus as Messiah meant that the Jews were replaced by Christianity. Paul was a Jew and Christianity as we now know it was still in the future. No, Paul would argue (Romans 11) that the Jews were still God's people and that they still had a part in God's plans.

> **Colossians 1:27**
> **"to whom God willed to make known what is the riches of the glory of this mystery among the**

*Gentiles, which is Christ in you, the hope of glory."*

This short precise of Paul focuses on the declaration, that the inclusion of the Gentiles is God's will. This is no verse to be quickly passed over for us who are Gentiles - we who were 'no hopers' have become 'glorious hopers'! Paul wrote of Gentiles:

> *"remember that you were at that time separate from Christ, excluded from the commonwealth of Israel, and strangers to the covenants of promise, having no hope and without God in the world." (Ephesians 2:12)*

This is the staggering truth. Gentiles had no hope outside of Jesus. We were excluded from the Messiah according to the interpretation of the Jewish Scriptures. We had no knowledge of the covenants of promise. We would never have known of these, except that God had plans and purposes to reveal them to us. This is the amazing grace of God at work. His actions in the life of Paul were the actions of a God going beyond the thinking of man. He set aside Paul to tell the Gentiles what was hidden in the Jewish Scriptures and now revealed in Jesus the Messiah. Not only was the door of salvation revealed to us but also access to the 'glorious riches' of this mystery we have discussed above. These glorious riches are elsewhere referred to:

- The kindness, tolerance, patience of God. (Rom. 2:4)

- We have become the people of God. (Rom. 9:23ff.)
- We have Salvation. (Rom. 10:12-13)
- Access to the wisdom and knowledge of God. (Rom. 11:33)
- Grace, from which we have redemption and forgiveness. (Eph. 1:7)
- The inheritance of the saints. (Eph. 1:18)
- Kindness towards us in Christ Jesus. (Eph.2:7)
- God will supply all our needs. (Phil. 4:19)

Add to that, what Paul points to: Christ is us and the hope of Glory. Truly they are glorious riches!

This Christ in us is referring to the Spirit of Christ. Paul spells this out in Romans:

> *"However, you are not in the flesh but in the Spirit, if indeed the Spirit of God dwells in you but if anyone does not have the Spirit of Christ, he does not belong to Him. If Christ is in you, though the body is dead because of sin, yet the spirit is alive because of righteousness. But if the Spirit of Him who raised Jesus from the dead dwells in you, He who raised Christ Jesus from the dead will also give life to your mortal bodies through His Spirit who dwells in you." (Romans 8:9-11)*

We see that we know we are of God because of the witness of the Holy Spirit within us. This is our security and our certain hope. This same Spirit will also give us life after death. This is Paul's great encouragement to the Colossians and through the Spirit to us. We live now in Christ; Christ, through His Spirit, lives in us - that same Spirit is our seal and pledge and it is He who will quicken our mortal bodies after death to make them into the new bodies promised in Scripture (Rom 8:23; 1 Cor 15:42). In our new bodies we will spend eternity with Christ in glory.

### Colossians 1:28

*"We proclaim Him, admonishing every man and teaching every man with all wisdom, so that we may present every man complete in Christ."*

If there is any such thing as Biblical Counselling, then this verse is its definition. Firstly, note what is proclaimed - the summary of all that which is preached or taught, especially in the Gospel, is Jesus Christ. He must be the focus and reason for everything a Christian speaks. The Holy Spirit's work within every believer is to draw attention to Jesus. He is the ultimate answer to every question asked about life. Any counsel to any human being about life here and hereafter, can only be effective if it points to Jesus as the answer. And how should we proceed to inform others? As has already pointed out above, Paul uses the Greek word '*noutheteo*'. This is used only eight times in Scripture in this form and is usually translated, 'admonish' or 'warn'. Its true sense is this idea of counselling someone that the path they are on is dangerous and they need to do something about it. It is as if you found someone walking close towards a cliff edge. There is no use giving a lecture on the dangers of walking close to cliff edges, but there is a need to give an urgent call of warning to avoid their falling over the edge. Three times Paul uses 'every man'; this is a generic term for both men and women. All people need this urgent warning. They have to be warned of the danger they face of eternal hell, of eternal separation from God.

Having warned them there then is the need to instruct them, to give them good doctrine, as the sense of the word is. Doctrine is often considered a dirty word in certain circles, but for Paul it was a vital matter. Paul is writing in a situation where heresy is threatened and his provocation is to warn and then to teach sound doctrine. Elsewhere he writes:

> *"For the time will come when they will not endure sound doctrine; but wanting to have their ears tickled, they will accumulate for themselves teachers in accordance to their own desires," (2 Timothy 4:3)*

In these days particularly, there is a need to make sure that we hold fast to sound doctrine, inspired from the Word of God, by the Holy Spirit. The teaching is to be with 'wisdom'. This is not the wisdom of the world but the gift of wisdom from the Holy Spirit. Any counsel ever given must have at its heart, the inspiration of the Spirit that directs men to solve their problems in the light of Christ. This is because all men and woman must be presented to Christ and they are to be 'complete' or more accurately, 'mature' as the word means here. Again, Paul expands this elsewhere:

*"until we all attain to the unity of the faith, and of the knowledge of the Son of God, to a mature man, to the measure of the stature which belongs to the fullness of Christ." (Ephesians 4:13)*

In this passage we are reading of the equipping of the saints, being built into a spiritual body, where maturity is marked by unity of faith, and the growing knowledge of the Son of God, Jesus Christ. The aim is to mature into the stature of that same Jesus. All who would preach or teach must have as their aim this principle of warning and turning people around to follow Jesus (Preaching) and then maturing them as saints of the Lord (Teaching). Then indeed, all will be able to stand on that awesome day, when the Messiah returns.

*Colossians 1:29*
*"For this purpose, also I labour, striving according to His power, which mightily works within me."*

This verse could be rendered literally from the Greek, as follows:

"This is the goal for which I exhaust myself. I agonizingly strive with the help of His powerful energy that is working in me."

This is Paul's attitude to the preaching of the Gospel and the maturing of Christians. He is no armchair evangelist, with dreams of doing something; he is a called man, filled with the power of the Spirit. He agonises over his work, striving, not in his own strength, but in the power of God within him. Paul is a man who wrestles in prayer, fighting like a gladiator, for every soul. He is able to endure so much, not because he is strong in himself, but it is in Paul's weaknesses that God can exercise His power through Paul. Think of a body of people so unified and so committed as Paul here. What could they do in God's hands? In such a situation, the early Disciples turned the world upside down! (Acts 17:6)

# Chapter Two

***Colossians 2:1***

***"I want you to know how great a struggle I have on your behalf and for those who are at Laodicea, and for all those who have not personally seen my face,"***

Paul picks up from the previous verse and whilst Paul did struggle and work hard for the Gospel in a general sense, he now personalizes it to the Colossians and Laodiceans. Remember that Colossae was located close to Laodicea, and this area was a hotbed of heretical activity. The forces of course were not simply flesh and blood, but the unseen powers of the kingdom of darkness. The word translated 'struggle' here, is the root of 'agony' again. But here it means to 'contest' or 'fight' as a gladiator. It reflects Paul's writing elsewhere:

*"I fought with wild beasts at Ephesus.." 1*
*Cor 15:32*

Paul's experience of spreading the Gospel was an experience of war (1Thes 2:2; 1Tim 6:12; 2Tim 4:7). He had to face down heresy and corruption of the Gospel wherever he went. This was no less so at Colossae; on their behalf Paul had so wrestled. Not only for those at Colossae, but also those at the nearby Laodicea. The next phrase does not mean Paul had never visited Colossae or Laodicea, because he had visited this area (Acts 18:23) and was acquainted with some of its members (Epaphras and Philemon). But Paul is expressing concern for those who had never met him personally or had never heard him preach. He was stressing that his love and affection was not simply to those he had personal relationship with, but for all who followed the Messiah. Such is the true Christian heart, which sees in all God's family, brothers and sisters, whether known personally or not. Brothers and sisters for whom there is to be a willingness to lay down one's life and to fight on their behalf. Surely Paul was living out the command of his, and our, Master:

> *"This is My commandment, that you love*
> *one another, just as I have loved you. Greater*
> *love has no one than this that one lay down his*
> *life for his friends." (John 15:12-13)*

**Colossians 2:2**
**"that their hearts may be encouraged, having**
**been knit together in love, and attaining to all**
**the wealth that comes from the full assurance**
**of understanding, resulting in a true knowledge**
**of God's mystery, that is, Christ Himself,"**

Here Paul sets out his goal for being willing to fight for them. He wants every heart 'encouraged'. The word here is from the same root for the Holy Spirit, the comforter. The encouragement between Christians is to be a comfort one to another. To be prepared at any cost to get alongside a fellow believer and stand with them. This flows from what God has done. He has 'knit' together the believers. This is reflected in Paul writing elsewhere:

*"from whom the whole body, being fitted*
*and held together by what every joint supplies,*
*according to the proper working of each*
*individual part, causes the growth of the body*
*for the building up of itself in love."*
*(Ephesians 4:16)*

This is part of the encouragement and comfort; that every part of the body is in place, according to God's design. When you are in battle, each soldier has been given a duty. For some it is advancing against the enemy. Others may be in rear-guard action, protecting any attack from behind. Some may be behind enemy lines, destroying communications etc. If each soldier can truly rely on his brother soldier, then he can fight with greater confidence. That is why the body will grow and be built up in the strength of the commanding officer Jesus.

Note too, that this knitting and working together is in love. This is the hallmark that others should see in a Christian body. How they care and contend for one another. How they sacrifice themselves for one another in both small and great ways. This is how the world knows they belong to the Messiah (John 13:35). The rendering 'attaining to'

(NASB) in this verse, is to communicate that what follows flows from the unity of the knitting together. The unity of love creates the conditions of blessing. This echoes the well-known Psalm's words:

> *A Song of Ascents, of David.*
>
> *How good and how pleasant it is for brothers*
> *to dwell together in unity! It is like the precious*
> *oil upon the head, coming down upon the beard,*
> *even Aaron's beard, coming down upon the edge*
> *of his robes. It is like the dew of Hermon coming*
> *down upon the mountains of Zion; for there the*
> *LORD commanded the blessing--life forever."*
>
> *(Psalms 133:1-3)*

This is the song of the priests as they ascend the steps to sacrifice at the Temple. We are the Royal Priests, brought into being by Jesus. We are dressed in festal robes, and upon them is poured the drenching of the Holy Spirit. Like the dew of Hermon, it brings refreshment and delight. In their unity, is released the blessing, life forever!

Paul goes onto to speak of that which is attained; 'a wealth that comes from a full assurance of understanding'. Before the wealth is received, there needs to be a full assurance or confidence. This is speaking of a true sound foundation of faith, which knows the truth of the Gospel - a confidence in the person and work of Christ. The understanding Paul is speaking off is an intellectual grasp, in the mind, that is informed by the Spirit. (See Romans 12:1) This is where knowledge is stored. The word Paul uses is '*epignosis*'. The secret knowledge (*gnosis*) of the heresy at Colossae was destructive. The true knowledge of Jesus must fill the mind. It is to know the true revealed mystery as discussed earlier, that the Messiah had come in Jesus to bring salvation to all men, both Jew and Greek. As noted above, this was the amazing revelation Paul had had. This is how heresy must be dealt with; the Spirit-filled life will take all things that enter the mind captive to Christ and discern if it is of the Lord.

With the Holy Spirit, the Word of God and the gift of discernment, the believer will be well equipped to deal with any attempts to draw them away from the living God. The belonging to a unified body of true believers - also relying on the Holy Spirit, Word of God and discernment, will also be a bulwark against the enemy.

*Colossians 2:3*

*"in whom are hidden all the treasures of wisdom and knowledge."*

Paul is again referring to the heresy at Colossae where forces were suggesting they had the secret *gnosis* or knowledge. Paul points to Jesus where the true wisdom and knowledge was hidden. In the Targum of Jonathan translation, we find the expression '*and the pathways of the luminaries; and thence are the treasures of the wisdom*'. This is speaking of Exodus 40 in which is the description of the inner holy of holies and the tabernacle. This place was 'hidden' and the *menorah* light was to illuminate the area outside the veil. It stood with the bread.

The Ark of the Covenant was 'hidden' behind the veil. Jesus the Light of the world and the Bread of Life had torn the veil in two (Mark 15:38). Now all had free access to the Holy of Holies, through the knowledge and faith in Jesus.

In the letter to the Colossians Paul has spoken of the cosmic Christ who was at the beginning and caused all things to be made. Paul is equating Jesus the Messiah with Wisdom (1 Corinthians 1:30). As we saw in the expansion of this thought in Ephesians, Paul links this to the mystery of Christ:

> *"and to bring to light what is the administration of the mystery which for ages has been hidden in God who created all things; so that the manifold wisdom of God might now be made known through the church to the rulers and the authorities in the heavenly places. This was in accordance with the eternal purpose which He carried out in Christ Jesus our Lord",*
> *Eph 3:9-1*

Paul's Jewish understanding believed that Wisdom was eternal and was before all things. Paul's revelation was that Jesus the Messiah was now that Wisdom embodied in flesh. The heretical wisdom that was tempting the Colossians was false. The eternal Wisdom of God was in

Christ Jesus. He was the Light that guided men and was the Bread that sustained them. He was the one who had opened up the way into the Holy of Holies and had in His death given access to the hidden treasure of the Ark. That is the mercy and grace of God now available to all men. Paul wrote to the Corinthians:

> *"For indeed Jews ask for signs and Greeks search for wisdom; but we preach Christ crucified, to Jews a stumbling block and to Gentiles foolishness, but to those who are the called, both Jews and Greeks, Christ the power of God and the wisdom of God. Because the foolishness of God is wiser than men, and the weakness of God is stronger than men." (1Co 1:22-25)*

It is foolishness to try and exist outside of Jesus Christ. The wisest person is the one who recognises Jesus and embraces Him for eternal life. The veil has been removed and the way open, there is no need of any 'secret' knowledge or need of a guru to lead us to God. Jesus has done all necessary to give us access to God and to His Holy Spirit who imparts to the children of God all necessary wisdom and knowledge.

**Colossians 2:4**
**"I say this so that no one will delude you with persuasive argument"**

Paul has been making oblique references to the heresy at Colossae. Now he directly warns the readers. His reasons for what he has said to this point are to protect the believers. The image here is of a good shepherd The Middle Eastern shepherd would make sure that the pasture where sheep were to feed has been cleared of snakes or wild beasts. Anything that would harm sheep must be dealt with severely. The wolves were at Colossae and were threatening the sheep. If successful they would delude and ravage the flock there. They were very persuasive and cunning. Their arguments sounded right and proper that even the elect might be deceived. Later Paul will make more specific comments, but for now he simply warns against this mix of religious heresy, that brought together Jewish, Greek and Oriental religions into a dangerous deception. Even today the Christian must be on guard against such deceptions that have always plagued the people of God. Indeed, as Paul was inspired to write elsewhere:

*"For such men are false Apostles, deceitful workers, disguising themselves as Apostles of Christ. No wonder, for even Satan disguises himself as an angel of light. Therefore, it is not surprising if his servants also disguise themselves as servants of righteousness, whose end will be according to their deeds." (2 Corinthians 11:13-15)*

*Colossians 2:5*

*"For even though I am absent in body, nevertheless I am with you in spirit, rejoicing to see your good discipline and the stability of your faith in Christ."*

Paul is writing from a Roman imprisonment. He cannot be physically present with the Colossians. However, their relationship is in Christ and he is with them in spirit. Such it is with all the children of God: their spirits are as one in Christ - when one suffers, Paul says, all suffer and when one weeps, all weep. (Romans 12:15). In their spiritual danger, Paul is with them in prayer and exhortation to remain faithful to Jesus. Not only this, Paul rejoices with them, because the heresy has not yet taken hold among them. They are disciplined and solid in their faith. The Greek terms being used by Paul are military. He is observing the Roman soldiers around him. (Phil 1:13) They were an amazing fighting machine; they remain ordered and ranked and steadfast in battle. This was to be how the Church behaved in the face of the enemy. They were to remain in their 'ranks', solid in the defence of the truth and fighting together against the forces of deception. Their faith was not in the flesh, but in Christ. Twice elsewhere Paul speaks of putting on the armour for the battle: He was the Commanding Officer. His word was truth and life. They were to avoid anything that drew them away from Him. This is to be the way with all believers. They are to be so in fellowship in Christ that they support and defend each other and seek to prevent any brother or sister falling into deception. James wrote:

> *"My brethren, if any among you strays from the truth and one turns him back, let him know that he who turns a sinner from the error of his way will save his soul from death and will cover a multitude of sins." (James 5:19-20)*

## Colossians 2:6
### *"Therefore, as you have received Christ Jesus the Lord, so walk in Him,"*

With the linking 'therefore', Paul points them back to their acceptance of Christ - 'as you have received' – this is to describe an action in the past, but which continues in the present. In John 5:43, Jesus speaks to the crowd and, as He stands physically with them, declares they will not 'receive' Him. In this He is indicating that they would not accept His authority as Lord and Saviour. Paul wrote elsewhere:

> "that if you confess with your mouth Jesus as Lord, and believe in your heart that God raised Him from the dead, you will be saved;" (Romans 10:9)

You cannot separate the salvation of Christ from accepting His Lordship and authority. To receive Him by faith is to accept Him in all that He is as the Son of God and the Son of Man, who has been given all authority. This, the heretics of Colossae, would try to deny. The consequences of 'receiving' Jesus the Lord and the Messiah, was that the believer should walk in Him. This, for Paul, would be to walk after the Spirit of Christ and not the flesh. The believer is to walk in Him and furthermore, Paul makes clear that belonging to God rested on that same Spirit witnessing within the believer:

> *"However, you are not in the flesh but in the*
> *Spirit, if indeed the Spirit of God dwells in you*
> *but if anyone does not have the Spirit of Christ,*
> *he does not belong to Him." (Romans 8:9)*

When Paul uses the expression 'walk' here, he is again using it in the understanding of *Halakah* (To walk). *Halakah* is that Jewish way of life that is lived according to the ethical and spiritual principles of God, especially applied to Jesus' own teaching and principles. Paul is pointing clearly to these teachings and life exemplified by the Lord Jesus Christ. In this then the Colossians are to live out their lives in the Spirit of Christ and not wander off into dogmas and doctrines, taught by men.

### Colossians 2:7

**"having been firmly rooted and now being built up in Him and established in your faith, just as you were instructed, and overflowing with gratitude."**

71

Paul turns his metaphor from walking to being 'rooted'. The only other place in the NT where a similar usage is found is again by Paul:

*"so that Christ may dwell in your hearts through faith; and that you, being rooted and grounded in love," (Ephesians 3:17)*

Here is the duality of Christ being the One in whom we are rooted, but who also dwells in our hearts. It is also love in which we are rooted and we are pointed to the love of Christ, which was the motivation in God's heart when He sent His Son. (John 3:16) In the Ephesians' verse we are also pointed to faith, to which we will turn later. The language tense used by Paul is again speaking of a past event that is still continuing. In other words, the believer is not to look back to the past event when we were rooted in Christ, but to be aware that we must continually be rooted or, as elsewhere, abiding in, Christ. This idea of the believer as rooted or as a tree is not unusual in Scripture.

*"To grant those who mourn in Zion, giving them a garland instead of ashes, the oil of gladness instead of mourning, the mantle of praise instead of a spirit of fainting so they will be called oaks of righteousness, the planting of the LORD, that He may be glorified." Isa 61:3*

Isaiah brings home the heart of the Lord for His people of all time, Jew or Gentile. He has rescued them from the dust, giving them the Holy

Spirit (oil), as a praising people, they are to be well-rooted oaks of righteousness, to demonstrate the glory of God. So here at Colossae, the people were to be well rooted and not swayed by the heresy or teaching of men.

Paul continues and changes the metaphor again; they are to be continually built up - present ongoing tense. Their building is not in themselves, but in Him. They are both rooted and being built up in Christ. He is the builder who is building the Church. (Matt 16:18) If He is not the one building, we labour in vain. (Psalm 127:1) Then Paul points them to faith. They are to be 'established' that is 'confirmed' or 'stabilised' in their faith. The meaning is dual in that by their possessing faith they are strengthened and by the faith (fullness) of Christ they are also strengthened. Whilst it is always the faith (fullness) of Christ that sustains us, by exercising our faith we are also established. We are called to an active faith life that demonstrates itself in a life of stepping out, at the call of God, to hear and obey Him. This is the true meaning of the Hebrew word 'hear' - *shema* - that is to hear and to do. Furthermore, this faith is centred on Christ and the Gospel as Epaphras had taught them. The apostolic authority of Paul endorsed him and what was taught was in line with the Scriptures and doctrines as handed down. Paul urged the Thessalonians:

> *"So then, brethren, stand firm and hold to the*
> *traditions which you were taught, whether by*

*word of mouth or by letter from us." (2*
*Thessalonians 2:15)*

He also instructs Titus in his ministry to those who would be Elders:

*"holding fast the faithful word which is in*
*accordance with the teaching, so that he will be*
*able both to exhort in sound doctrine and to*
*refute those who contradict." (Titus 1:9)*

This is why we read at the time of Pentecost when the Spirit comes in power; one thing that the believers were devoted to, was the apostolic teaching. (Acts 2:42) The Colossians were not to depart from the Word of God as taught by Paul and others. We too in our day and age must also be alert to any doctrine that is opposed to the revealed apostolic teaching of Scripture. The words of Jesus Himself warn us from the prophet Isaiah:

*"in vain do they worship me, teaching as*
*doctrines the commandments of men" (Matthew*
*15:9)*

At Colossae this was exactly what was happening and Paul is encouraging them, and us, to remain rooted in Christ, established in faith in Him and to stick to the revealed Scriptures. All of this was to be done with joy in overflowing gratitude to God. Paul has already outlined to his readers, what God has done in Christ. They are to rejoice and be grateful in that and not depart from these truths to the heresy of men that would eventually enslave them, if not rejected.

*Colossians 2:8*

*"See to it that no one takes you captive through philosophy and empty deception, according to the tradition of men, according to the elementary principles of the world, rather than according to Christ."*

Paul is using a term that is suggesting robbers who steal and kidnap. This process would turn the victim into a slave, no longer free. Paul is directly addressing the heresy and its teachers. They are thieves and robbers who would come to steal away the treasures that the Colossians had gained in Christ. They would do it through 'philosophy'. This is the only place this term is used in the Early Church Texts and it must have been a central element in the heresy. The word means a 'lover of wisdom'. Indeed, it was a feature of Greek society to search out wisdom and new things:

*"For indeed Jews ask for signs and Greeks search for wisdom;" (1 Corinthians 1:22)*

Paul's use here is more specific in that he is referring to a form of Judaism which became absorbed in detailed, speculative enquiry into the nature and classes of angels, rituals and the Mosaic Law regulations of Jewish tradition on practical life. Paul is not arguing against reason or scientific enquiry but is rather arguing that it must be a servant of the mind not its master. Christ was to be that Master to our reason and all thoughts were to be brought captive to Him. This he makes clear to the Corinthians:

> *"We are destroying speculations and every lofty thing raised up against the knowledge of God, and we are taking every thought captive to the obedience of Christ," (2 Corinthians 10:5)*

Paul is making clear that his readers must hold fast to the teachings as delivered to them and not be seduced by fancy and novel doctrines. Elsewhere he had warned Timothy:

> *"For the time will come when they will not endure sound doctrine; but wanting to have their ears tickled, they will gather up, for themselves, teachers in accordance to their own desires," (2 Timothy 4:3)*

This is the warning to avoid the teaching that departs from apostolic authority, to teachings that are no more than empty deception. The words Paul uses mean 'vain delusion'. Thereby Paul is pointing to teaching that seeks knowledge for its own sake and makes for arrogance (1 Cor 8:1). To think you have superior knowledge about matters or to seek after teachings that will confirm your own arrogance or sense of being one of the elite is no more than a vain illusion.

Furthermore, Paul calls it 'elementary'; that is to say, it is like a child's learning the A, B, C. These elementary principles were in fact childish foolishness not true spiritual wisdom. To accept this false teaching is to go into bondage as Paul wrote to the Galatians:

*"So also we, while we were children, were held in*
*bondage under the elemental things of the world."*
*(Galatians 4:3)*

Later Paul will spell out in more detail these matters, but for now we are called to take heed to Paul's warning, less we too go into such slavery. Rather we are to conform to Christ who has set us free. Paul has already written to the Colossians making plain that they had been delivered from the kingdom of darkness and the domain of slavery and had been transferred to the Kingdom of God's beloved Son. (Col 1:13). They were now to conform to Him in all matters. In the next verse Paul makes plain why.

### Colossians 2:9
### *"For in Him all the fullness of Deity dwells in bodily form,"*

This is one of the most crucial verses in the whole Scripture as to the nature of Christ. Paul uses two expressions here found in this form, nowhere else in the Early Church Texts. They are 'Godhead' (Deity) and 'Bodily form'. All heresy and false religion will attack the nature of Christ either denying His divine nature or His human nature. But here Paul spells out very clearly the truth of the nature of Christ. Whilst all the knowledge and will and attributes of God no doubt were Christ's, Paul is not meaning these things here. Rather he is inspired to write that the very God Himself is the nature of Christ. Any religion or philosophy that would deny that Christ by nature is God, is denying the truth of this verse. Furthermore, this nature exists in a human body. In other words, the divine is revealed in human form. This great mystery of God is beyond our knowledge, the heresy and philosophy in its arguments would want to explain it away by human wisdom. This is why Paul's readers must not be taken captive by deception. The only way man could be rescued from his situation was by the Divine becoming human and in that perfection be the perfect acceptable sacrifice for sin. To reject that would be to reject Christ and the means of salvation, which would lead to death and separation from God. We can hear this echoed in Paul's great hymn in Philippians:

> *"Have this attitude in yourselves which was also in Christ Jesus, who, although He existed in the form of God, did not regard equality with God a thing to be grasped, but emptied Himself, taking the form of a bond-servant, and being made in the likeness of men. Being found in appearance as a man, He humbled Himself by becoming obedient to the point of death, even death on a cross. For this reason also, God highly exalted Him, and bestowed on Him the*

*name which is above every name, so that at the*
*name of Jesus EVERY KNEE WILL BOW, of*
*those who are in heaven and on earth and under*
*the earth, and that every tongue will confess that*
*Jesus Christ is Lord, to the glory of God the*
*Father." (Philippians 2:5-11)*

What a mystery to be worshipped, not questioned. That God Himself should lay aside His majesty and enter into our world so that we may know His righteousness, love and holiness for ourselves. Hallelujah!

**Colossians 2:10**
**"and in Him you have been made complete, and**
**He is the head over all rule and authority";**

Because of who Christ is and what He has done, Paul encourages the believers that in Him, in Christ, they have been made complete, or perfect, as the word can mean. This is part of the mystery of the work of Christ. The human being who believes in Him by faith is not changed physically. Neither is he (or she) free from the sin that can so easily entangle. The believer exists in a world where temptation and distractions and all sorts of other impediments to faith exist. In ourselves we can be are weak and often faithless. Yet despite all this, because of their sincere declaration of faith in the nature and work of Jesus, they are here, in Scripture, declared 'perfect' in Christ. The language does not mean future but is a present reality. This is the state of the believer in Christ. He is being covered by the righteousness of Jesus, whilst the transforming work of the Holy Spirit is changing him from glory to glory. As Paul states elsewhere:

*"But we all, with unveiled face, beholding as*

*in a mirror the glory of the Lord, are being*

*transformed into the same image from glory to*

*glory, just as from the Lord, the Spirit."*

*(2 Corinthians 3:18)*

In this we are called to look into the glorious Gospel of Jesus Christ. In that Gospel we see ourselves transformed by the of God and placed into Christ. His radiance we see reflected in us, as we have become the righteousness of God (2 Cor 5:21). This is a Hebraism for 'divine righteousness'. Whilst covered in that righteousness, the work of the Spirit leads us on to become more like Christ, until that day when we are presented by Christ to Himself (Ephesians 5:27), when we collectively, in Paul's analogy, .."He might present the church to himself in splendour, without spot or wrinkle or any such thing, that she might be holy and without blemish" ready for the eternal joy of union with our Saviour! This is the future hope, but also the present reality - that in Christ we are perfected. On the cross the great exchange was made; Jesus took our filthy rags of sin and gave to us His robe of righteousness. This is the scene reflected in Zec 3:3-4, when Joshua is taken out of accusation by Satan and placed in festival robes. That is why Paul can write of a truth:

*"Therefore, there is now no condemnation for*
*those who are in Christ Jesus." (Romans 8:1)*

Furthermore, as was stated earlier, Jesus is the final authority. No traditions of men can declare us perfect. The philosophy of Greece and the traditions of the Jews could not bring us such perfection. No other authority could declare us fit for the Kingdom of God. It is only through the authority and Word of Christ have we been qualified (1 Col 12) for the position we now hold in Christ. The heresy that Paul is referring to was some distorted doctrine that was requiring a physical mark as qualification is seen in the following verse.

### Colossians 2:11

**"and in Him you were also circumcised with a circumcision made without hands, in the removal of the body of the flesh by the circumcision of Christ;"**

The false teachers at Colossae were teaching that the mark of circumcision, that is the removal of a small piece of flesh, was the essential key to enter into the covenant of Christ. Paul is refuting this in a very strong way. He will look at baptism to explain the inclusion into Christ, but here, he makes a far bolder statement. It is not simply a small piece of a foreskin that has been, or needs to be, removed; rather it is the whole body of flesh that needs dealing with to be in Christ. This body of flesh is an internal matter of the heart and can only be performed by the Spirit not a human hand. Paul wrote to the Romans:

> *"But he is a Jew who is one inwardly; and circumcision is that which is of the heart, by the Spirit, not by the letter; and his praise is not from men, but from God." (Romans 2:29)*

As we will see later, in Baptism, the believer puts off the flesh or 'old man' – he crucifies it - as Scripture says.

> *"Now those who belong to Christ Jesus have crucified the flesh with its passions and desires." (Galatians 5:24)*

And Paul writes in Romans:

> *"For if we have become united with Him in the likeness of His death, certainly we shall also be in the likeness of His resurrection," (Romans 6:5)*

In this Paul is pointing to the circumcision of Christ. That is Jesus lived out His life as a human being. (Philippians 2:5-11) When He was crucified and buried, His physical body was laid in the tomb. (John 19:40-42) In the resurrection, that physical body was transformed into a heavenly body and it was in that body, that Jesus was raised from the dead. (John 20:19: Roman's 6:9; Phil 3:20-2: Heb 10:10) Although Jesus was raised in a heavenly body, He still bore the scars of death. This He did not need to do. That same Spirit that raised Jesus from the dead could have removed all trace of the suffering endured. However, the scars remained as evidence that this was the same man that went into death and came out. Thomas saw these marks and with the realisation that Jesus was not now limited by walls and could appear in the midst at will, declared 'My Lord and my God'. (John 20:28) These scars were also evident to John, who when He sees the heavenly vision records:

> "And I saw between the throne (with the four living
> creatures) and the elders a Lamb standing, as if slain,
> (Revelation 5:6 a)

When Jesus returns the Jews too will see the scars and they too will realise this was the same man that was crucified and who had walked the earth. (Zec 12:10) When a believer enters into Christ by faith, he too is transformed and he becomes a spiritual being (2 Cor 5:6-8; Phil 1:20-24) who will also receive a new body, which is the same as that of Christ's, at the resurrection (Romans 8:23; 1 Cor 15:42-58 (Note v42 & 44); 2 Cor 4:10-14; 1 Thes 5:23). A human being cannot do any of this work; it is a sovereign work of the Holy Spirit. The believer is to abide in Christ and to accept the gift of the Holy Spirit. Paul writes:

> "For God has not given us a spirit of timidity,
> but of power and love and discipline." (2 Timothy
> 1:7)

With the removal of the body of flesh the believer is to co-operate with the Holy Spirit in bringing the passions of the flesh under control. Paul again writes:

*"Do you not know that those who run in a race all run, but only one receives the prize? Run in such a way that you may win. Everyone who competes in the games exercises self-control in all things they then do it to receive a perishable wreath, but we an imperishable. Therefore, I run in such a way, as not without aim; I box in such a way, as not beating the air; but I discipline my body and make it my slave, so that, after I have preached to others, I myself will not be disqualified." (1 Corinthians 9:24-27)*

There is interesting light shed on this in Acts:

*"But as he (Paul) was discussing righteousness, self-control and the judgment to come, Felix became afraid and said, "Go away for the time being, and when I find time I will call you back." (Acts 24:25)*

It is interesting what the Spirit inspires Luke to write here. We are told of three things that Paul is sharing with this official. Firstly; righteousness, which Paul taught came through Christ by faith; secondly, self-control that the believer exercises whilst in the physical body and thirdly: judgement that awaits every man and woman who has not confessed Christ as Lord and Saviour. It is no wonder Felix was afraid because as we read on in that portion of Scripture we see he certainly had not had the body of flesh removed.

*Colossians 2:12*

*"having been buried with Him in baptism, in which you were also raised up with Him through faith in the working of God, who raised Him from the dead."*

Paul continues this theme of circumcision by the Spirit by linking it to baptism. In this we are brought to see that baptism is not a mere symbol but has an amazing spiritual reality. For Paul spiritual circumcision is baptism. It might be helpful to point out that at the time of Paul, repentance and faith in Christ was immediately followed by baptism during which the evidence of the seal of the Holy Spirit was given. The rite of baptism was simple in that the believer, after a confession of faith, immersed himself completely beneath the water, and was entering the grave, signifying the death of self. Following this he arose from the waters and entered into a new resurrected life. The thorny question needs to be faced as to the necessity of believer's baptism for salvation. Let us look at some texts:

> *"Jesus answered, "Truly, truly, I say to you, unless one is born of water and the Spirit he cannot enter into the kingdom of God." (John 3:5)*

This is strong evidence from the Master Himself, that being 'born of water' (baptism?), is necessary for entrance to God's Kingdom.

> *"Peter said to them, "Repent, and each of you be*
> *baptised in the name of Jesus Christ for the*
> *forgiveness of your sins; and you will receive the gift*
> *of the Holy Spirit." (Acts 2:38)*

Here Peter includes baptism in the name of Jesus Christ as being 'for the forgiveness of sins'.

> *'Now why do you delay? Get up and be baptised,*
> *and wash away your sins, calling on His name.'*
> *(Acts 22:16)*

Paul's own testimony here speaks of his being commanded to 'be baptised and wash away your sins'.

> *"He saved us, not on the basis of deeds which we*
> *have done in righteousness, but according to His*
> *mercy, by the washing of regeneration and renewing*
> *by the Holy Spirit," (Titus 3:5)*

It would be a mistake here to think that 'the washing of regeneration' i.e. baptism was a means of regeneration. Regeneration is the act of the Sprit, but it appears, in this verse, that in the Biblical pattern, this occurs during baptism. In which we are told He has 'saved us'.

> *"Corresponding to that, baptism now saves you-*
> *-not the removal of dirt from the flesh, but an appeal*
> *to God for a good conscience--through the*
> *resurrection of Jesus Christ" (1 Peter 3:21)*

Here Peter makes a clear statement in referring to Noah's flood, which immersed everything (except that which was on the ark) that it corresponded to baptism, which 'now saves you'; in that in baptism we are raised in Christ – He is the Ark that carries us through to safety.

In the Scriptural formula we find that, in the main, the person is called to repent, believe be baptised and receive the Holy Spirit. The baptism proceeds from faith. Therefore, the faith in baptism appears to be an essential element in the progress of the believer, which must be entered into, unless there are extreme circumstances that prevent it. In Paul's great epistle to the Romans, he lays out his Spirit inspired teaching on baptism, which helps us gain insight to his statement here in Colossians:

*"What shall we say then? Are we to continue in sin so that grace may increase? May it never be! How shall we who died to sin still live in it? Or do you not know that all of us who have been baptised into Christ Jesus have been baptised into His death? Therefore, we have been buried with Him through baptism into death, so that as Christ was raised from the dead through the glory of the Father, so we too might walk in newness of life. For if we have become united with Him in the likeness of His death, certainly we shall also be in the likeness of His resurrection, knowing this, that our old self was*

*crucified with Him, in order that our body of sin might be done away with, so that we would no longer be slaves to sin; for he who has died is freed from sin. Now if we have died with Christ, we believe that we shall also live with Him, knowing that Christ, having been raised from the dead, is never to die again; death no longer is master over Him"* *(Romans 6:1-9)*

This is our great encouragement as believers. The Holy Spirit has sealed us who have repented and believed on Jesus and who have entered in baptism as we were brought into Christ. Our steps of faith have made us alive in Christ in which we have become the righteousness of God (2 Cor 5:21). And as we see in this verse here in Colossians, this is the working of God. Does this mean a person who has repented and believed on the Lord Jesus is not 'saved' until they enter into believer's baptism? My own conclusion is that they are saved by their confession of faith. The simplest statement as to salvation is probably Paul's:

*"that if you confess with your mouth Jesus as Lord, and believe in your heart that God raised Him from the dead, you will be saved;" (Romans 10:9)*

This was indeed the experience of the thief on the cross. (Luke 23:43) However, to express Jesus as Lord requires obedience and so every believer who has been capable of such a confession is also bound to submit to baptism, as was Peter's direction at Pentecost. In this way entering into Baptism is an outward sign of a deep inward spiritual reality of belief in resurrection and identification with Christ in His death. This step of faith in Baptism is matched by a spiritual action in which the body of flesh is 'put of' and the believer is equipped with the Spirit to walk the life of faith. In this it is much more than mere symbolism and should be approached in that spirit.

*Colossians 2:13*
**"When you were dead in your transgressions and the uncircumcision of your flesh, He made you alive together with Him, having forgiven us all our transgressions,"**

Paul expands his thoughts on these matters in his letter to the Ephesians:

*"Among them we too all formerly lived in the lusts of our flesh, indulging the desires of the flesh and of the mind, and were by nature children of wrath, even as the rest. But God, being rich in mercy, because of His great love with which He loved us, even when we were dead in our transgressions, made us alive together with Christ (by grace you have been saved), and raised us up with Him, and seated us with Him*

*in the heavenly places in Christ Jesus, so that in
the ages to come He might show the surpassing
riches of His grace in kindness toward us in
Christ Jesus." (Ephesians 2:3-7)*

This gives the reader an opportunity to reflect on what has actually happened to them spiritually. It might be helpful to note Paul's rabbinic background and understanding about human nature. It all starts with Adam. Paul taught that Adam was the one who brought death into the world:

*"Nevertheless, death reigned from Adam
until Moses, even over those who had not sinned
in the likeness of the offence of Adam, who is a
type of Him who was to come." (Romans 5:14)*

*"For as in Adam all die, so also in Christ all
will be made alive." (1 Corinthians 15:22)*

It is necessary to look at the offence of Adam to fully understand the human state. God had told Adam that to eat of the fruit would be an offence that would have serious consequences. The Scripture says:

*"but from the tree of the knowledge of good
and evil you shall not eat, for in the day that you
eat from it you will surely die."*

*(Genesis 2:17)*

In these verses we see man has the ability to choose to do good or to do evil. Choice was there and man was good (*Genesis 1:31*). In eating the fruit of the tree that was forbidden, their eyes would be opened and in that new knowledge would lead to a propensity to commit evil. Their nature would change. No longer would they be in union with God. (They would die – The term 'death' is in its root meaning is 'to be separated'. The definition is clarified in the Lexicon: "Death, then, in the OT means ultimate separation from God due to sin. And sin is any rebellion or lack of conformity to his holy will.") Adam continued to physically live, but the Spirit of God was taken from him and in this he was separated from God and was spiritually dead. (See also David in Psalm 51:11. David knew very well that he would spiritually die.)

In this separated state, the Jewish Paul would understand that two forces were now at war in man. They were known as the *yetzer ra* (evil inclination) and the *yetzer tov* (good inclination). Because of Adam, man was helpless without the Spirit of God and lived in a state of death, destined to be ever separated from God. This is what Romans 7 is about. The struggle within man is the two natures at war and man cannot win it.

A Pharisee like Paul, desiring purity, would struggle with the evil inclination and the *Shema*:

> *"You shall love the LORD your God with all*
> *your heart and with all your soul and with all*
> *your might." Deut. 6.5.*

The rabbinical commentary states:

"In truth [the point of the two *yods*] is as stated by R. Simeon b. Pazzi; for R. Simeon b. Pazzi said: Woe is me because of my Creator, woe is me because of my evil inclination [*yizri*]!"[1] It is also written "If you argue: "Is it not the Holy One who created the impulse to evil, of which it is written, 'The evil impulse of man's heart was evil from the time he was expelled from his mother's womb?' Who then can possibly make it good?"[2] We also find it written, "If God created the evil inclination, He also created the *Torah* as its antidote."[3]

When we combine these, we see that there is a cry of woe because of the condition of the evil inclination. There is also the concern for what will 'make it good'. Finally, there is the antidote – the *Torah*. Indeed, as we look at Romans 7 we find Paul's own cry of woe, "Wretched man that I am! Who will set me free from the body of this death?" (Rom 7:24) His solution is, 'Jesus Christ our Lord'. (Rom 7:25) In this we see the thoughts of Romans 7 as the thoughts of a rabbinic Paul, describing the struggle between the evil inclination the good inclination.

The Rabbinic background that influenced Paul needs careful understanding. When they say 'God created the 'evil inclination', what they mean is that God created the whole man and all that was in him. It was man's choice that allowed the evil inclination to be acted on, not

---

[1] *b. Ber.* 61a.

[2] *Avot d'Rabbi Natan* 16.

[3] *Baba Batra* 16a.

God's choice. He had laid down firmly to Adam, what he should do. This is why God told Adam NOT to eat of the tree of the knowledge of good and evil – to eat it would awaken the evil inclination (Gen 2:17) This would beset man and cause the ills the human race has suffered ever since. The ultimate antidote was indeed the Lord Jesus.

That is why we see him move to a differing view of the *Torah* (as Law) that was the antidote in the above rabbinic comments to a solution found in *Messiah* (Christ) to where the Law pointed. (Rom 10:4) This was Paul's amazing revelation, that circumcision and the Law could not make him alive again and deliver him from his terrible situation – dead in sin - separated from God. He wrote in Romans;

> *"For what the Law could not do, weak as it*
> *was through the flesh, God did: sending His Own*
> *Son in the likeness of sinful flesh and as an*
> *offering for sin, He condemned sin in the flesh,"*
> *(Romans 8:3)*

The cutting of a small piece of flesh was useless, man had to be spiritually raised from the dead and spiritually made alive again. The Law could not help, was Paul's conclusion, someone, that is God, had to act from outside man and deal with the problem. The word translated 'made alive', in the NASB here is better 'quickened', as this describes what happens when someone believes. We were dead in our transgressions, gripped in uncircumcision of the flesh (a phrase that is Jewish, meaning the evil inclination and impurity). It is in that helpless state that the Spirit quickens the individual and the opportunity is given to hear the Gospel through preaching, a testimony, a witnessing etc. or God directly breaking in, as with Paul himself. Like a shaft of light, the darkness is pierced and if responded to, the individual comes to see his wretched condition and comes to repentance and faith in Jesus. This was Paul's own personal experience on the Damascus Road.

As Paul writes in the Ephesians letter quoted above, it is a perfect and complete act of grace from God, with no merit in man. The amazement doesn't stop there because we are 'made alive with Christ' and are where He is. Because of this, spiritually we are now in reality seated in heavenly places. Furthermore, the act of God did not deal with a few of our sins, but dealt with all our sins, past, present and future. Like a rich treasure house, the store of grace is there and ready to flow when we fall:

> *"but if we walk in the Light as He Himself is in the Light, we have fellowship with one another, and the blood of Jesus His Son cleanses us from all sin. If we say that we have no sin, we are deceiving ourselves and the truth is not in us. If we confess our sins, He is faithful and righteous to forgive us our sins and to cleanse us from all unrighteousness. If we say that we have not sinned, we make Him a liar and His word is not in us." (1 John 1:7-10)*

Amazing grace how sweet the sound

That saved a wretch like me,

I once was lost, but now am found,

Was blind, but now I see!

*Colossians 2:14*

*"having cancelled out the certificate of debt consisting of decrees against us, which was hostile to us; and He has taken it out of the way, having nailed it to the cross."*

This is how it was all done. The language here is speaking of 'handwriting of ordinances', which is a legal phrase. Paul is speaking of a handwritten document of some sort that was against men. This may mean the *Torah* that was believed to have been written directly by God. (Exodus 32:16) Paul writes:

*"by abolishing in His flesh the enmity, which is the Law of commandments contained in ordinances, so that in Himself He might make the two into one new man, thus establishing peace,"*

*(Ephesians 2:15)*

Paul was not saying that the Law was finished. It still held authority over all who had not died to it in Christ (Romans 7:6). However, this good and holy thing –the Law – was the very instrument that exposed how terrible our sin is (Romans 7:13). The decrees of the Law were, in

| The Law of Moses |
| --- |
| According to the Rabbis |
| 1) NO idolatry |
| 2) No sexual immorality |
| 3) No Bloodshed |
| 4) No robbery |
| 5) No Blood (Or flesh with blood in it) |
| 6) No blasphemy |
| 7) Establish Courts of Law |

that sense, hostile to us. Paul could also be meaning that according to his Jewish understanding, there was "the writing of the debt"[4] which was a ledger in which was written all the sins of men and the subsequent punishment due for those sins. The implication of Paul's language is that mankind had also signed the debt certificate as an obligation to obey God. In Noah all mankind was represented and when he was given universal commands (Known as the Seven Laws of Noah), all men were to obey them.

This is also seen when God calls His people before Him, through Moses and they give assent to obey:

*"All the people answered together and said,*
*"All that the LORD has spoken we will do!" And*
*Moses brought back the words of the people to*
*the LORD." (Exodus 19:8)*

Both Gentile (In Noah) and Jew (Through Moses) are under obligation to God to obey Him. As in Adam, disobedience means death.

---

[4] *Tzeror Hammor, fol. 87. 1, 3.*

Whether it was the Law or the ledger of debt that stood against us the end result was the same, we must die as long as it is in force. When Jesus was on the cross, just before He died, He cried out "It is finished!". In John's Gospel the Greek for this is given as Τετέλεσται. In the Greco-Roman world a debt, especially for taxes – a legal demand,

when paid would have this word stamped on it. The debt was now cleared and the document was proof. Here is an example of such a documents. The ancient document is hard to read but it states in the first clause, τετελ(ώνηται)(\*) διὰ πύλ(ης) Σοκπ(ατου) Νήσο(υ)(\*), 'It is finished/terminated/completed through the gate of Soknope Island'. We can hold up our certificate stating 'It is finished at Calvary"! The Gospel was conveying to the readers of the first century, who would be aware of this practice, Jesus has satisfied all legal demands on sinners.

This is what Paul is saying, when Jesus was nailed to the cross, in a way, above His head there was held the 'handwriting of ordinances' against us. What Paul may be also referring to is the practice of Romans when crucifying a criminal; they would make plain the broken laws for which the criminal was dying. Christ was no criminal, but we were, and He was taking our place.

---

[5] W. M. Brashear, BGU XIII 2324.Additional Literature: Zur Datierung und Z. 8 vgl. P. J. Sijpesteijn, P.Customs S. 147 zu Nr. 138 = BL IX 32.

It also could mean that Jesus Himself was nailed to the cross by the will of the Father and 'written' on Him were our sins.

> *"and He Himself bore our sins in His body on the cross, so that we might die to sin and live to righteousness; for by His wounds you were healed." (1 Peter 2:24)*

The blessed Saviour went to the cross in our stead. He paid for our debts against God. God Himself had taken the debt out of the way and nailed it to the cross. No Jew or Roman were ultimately responsible for Jesus' death, it was an amazing act of grace and sacrifice of the Father. The shocking verse of Isaiah comes to mind again:

> *"But Yahweh was pleased to crush Him, putting Him to grief; If He would render Himself as a guilt offering, He will see His offspring, He will prolong His days, and the good pleasure of Yahweh will prosper in His hand." (Isaiah 53:10)*

There is nothing now in the way of any man, Jew or Greek, to prevent them coming to God - as Jesus cried out: "It is finished!" (John 19:30). He has made a way where there seemed to be no way! The cross of death for Jesus was life to us.

*Colossians 2:15*
*"When He had disarmed the rulers and*
*authorities, He made a public display of them,*
*having triumphed over them through Him."*

This is a very difficult verse to interpret from the Greek. It is not clear whether God or Christ is the subject of the verse. It is also not clear whether the last word should be 'it' or 'Him'. It is also not clear who is 'stripped' or 'disarmed'. The most attractive understanding is that it is Christ who is stripped or divested, as the word can mean, of something. If we return to Paul's argument from verse 11 and the circumcision of Christ, with the idea of removal, we can see according to the Scriptures,

> *"..........God sent forth His Son, born of a*
> *woman, born under the Law," (Galatians 4:4)*

Furthermore, Scripture teaches us:

> *"Or do you not know, brethren (for I am*
> *speaking to those who know the law [i.e. Jews]),*
> *that the law has jurisdiction over a person as*
> *long as he lives?" (Romans 7:1)*

Jesus was under the restraint of the law and was subject to it and its penalties. Now we know that Satan the head of the 'rulers and authorities' attempted to cause Jesus to sin (Luke 4:1-13). However, Jesus had lived out His life under the Law in perfection (Heb 4:15). Jesus was nailed to a cross and in that was literally stripped naked (the meaning of the Greek in this verse). He was an innocent victim, a pure Lamb, He had remained clean and without sin, no one could bring a charge against God's Elected Son. In this then He triumphed over His enemies on the cross and in death removed all the claims of the Law upon Him. He divested Himself of these things. The Law, sin and death could never have any claim on Him. The great reality is that all who would die with Him in His death are also in the same position. This is Paul's great argument in Romans referred to in the comments on verse 12 above, and also explains what is written here in this verse 15 of Colossians:

*"Therefore, we have been buried with Him through baptism into death, so that as Christ was raised from the dead through the glory of the Father, so we too might walk in newness of life. For if we have become united with Him in the likeness of His death, certainly we shall also be in the likeness of His resurrection, knowing this, that our old self was crucified with Him, in order* ***that our body of sin might be done away with,*** *so that we would no longer be slaves to sin; for he who has died is freed from sin. Now if we have died with Christ, we believe that we shall also live with Him, knowing that Christ, having been raised from the dead, is never to die again; death*

*no longer is master over Him. For the death that He died, He died to sin once for all; but the life that He lives, He lives to God. Even so consider yourselves to be dead to sin, but alive to God in Christ Jesus." (Romans 6:4-11)*

This is how we are made complete or perfect, in that the Law, sin and death has no longer any hold over us – it has been stripped away from us. In the triumph of Jesus, we also triumph and the amazing truth of the inspired Paul comes home to us:

*"But in all these things we overwhelmingly conquer through Him who loved us. For I am convinced that neither death, nor life, nor angels, nor principalities, nor things present, nor things to come, nor powers, nor height, nor depth, nor any other created thing, will be able to separate us from the love of God, which is in Christ Jesus our Lord." (Romans 8:37-39)*

### Colossians 2:16
**"Therefore no one is to act as your judge in regard to food or drink or in respect to a festival or a new moon or a Sabbath day."**

On the basis of those thing discussed above, Paul now declares the great freedom of the believers in Christ – they are no longer to live under Law. We must not have the mistaken idea that Paul is advocating lawlessness. The believer is now dead to the world and to the Law. Like a married woman who dies, in her death she is released from subjection to her husband. Not simply to his attitude, whether praise or condemnation, but to his entirety of being. And so it is with the believer, the law has no lordship, headship, dominion, authority, power or effect on the righteous in Christ. These things are now in the one to whom the believer is made alive and is joined. He, the Lord Jesus Christ, is now Lord, Head, King, Authority, power and indeed righteousness of the believer. Does this mean the believer is now free to live lawlessly? No this is Paul's great assertion:

> *"Do we then nullify the Law through faith?*
> *May it never be! On the contrary, we establish*
> *the Law." (Romans 3:31)*

The contrast Paul makes is between 'nullify' or 'make void', that is 'do away with', and 'establish' or 'stand in its right place' or 'to uphold its authority'. In this, faith is the means to righteousness apart from Law. The believer having died to the Law, is not making it void but establishing it in its right place to maintain its holy and good role, to bring home to men the evil of their sinful nature (Romans 7). The heretics who were trying to take captive the Colossians would bring them into the bondage of living under Law with all its consequences of failure and death. They would stand in judgement on the Colossians and declare them condemned because they did not observe the rituals and rules as they saw them. However, a judge can only enforce laws that are in government over a people, but in dying in Christ the Law had no longer jurisdiction over them:

> "Therefore, my brethren, you also were made
> to die to the Law through the body of Christ, so
> that you might be joined to another, to Him who
> was raised from the dead, in order that we might
> bear fruit for God." (Romans 7:4)

They were to let no man judge them. This was entirely in keeping with the Scriptures as we also read in Romans 14 (and other places), where Paul discusses the same matters. In Christ we are to live by the Spirit not the Law being free from all condemnation and the judgement of others (Romans 8).

### Colossians 2:17
**"Things which are a mere shadow of what is to come; but the substance (body or reality) belongs to Christ."**

Paul here is writing in a way that is deeper than that which appears on the surface. Firstly, there is a contrast between 'shadow' and 'substance'. The community of Israel existed with the conditional covenant of God, to obey the Mosaic Law. But that was never meant to be the permanent reality of what God wanted for the whole of mankind. It was but the shadow of something to come. This something was the revelation of Jesus the Messiah. The word rendered 'substance' here is 'soma', which means body, reality or substance. Here Paul has also in mind the 'body of Jesus'. This is made clearer in the book of Hebrews chapter 10.

We read:

> "For the Law, since it has only a shadow of
> the good things to come and not the very form of
> things, can never, by the same sacrifices which
> they offer continually year by year, make perfect
> those who draw near." (Hebrews 10:1)

Here the Mosaic Law is shown as inadequate to permanently deal with the problem of man's sin. That is why the writer goes on to write, quoting Psalm 40:6:

> "For this very reason when he came into the
> world, he said,
> "Sacrifice and offering you not want",
> But a body you did prepare for me" (Hebrews
> 10:5)

The writer of Hebrews expected his readers to know the Scripture quoted from the Tanach, which reads in full:

*"Sacrifice and meal-offering You have no delight in; my ears have You opened; burnt-offering and sin-offering have You not required".*

The Mosaic Law required specific sacrifices to deal with sin – mentioned here in the *Tanach* – an animal sacrifice for slaughter and a meal-offering of unleavened bread*"*. Here in Hebrews, we find that word 'soma', the body of Jesus that had been prepared to be the final sacrifice – the Lamb – the un-leavened bread (Bread of Life) to deal with man's sin problem - permanently. The 'shadow' of the Mosaic Law was always pointing to the 'body' of Jesus as the true reality that would be sacrificed to bring salvation to man – something that the Mosaic Law could not do.

Finally, the 'body' of Christ is also the Church that has been purchased by the blood of Christ. That body by definition belongs to Jesus. It is under His authority and command. It is not under the authority or command of the Mosaic Law. This is exactly what Paul wrote to the Romans:

*"Therefore, my brethren, you also were made to die to the Law through the body (soma) of Christ, so that you might be joined to another, to Him who was raised from the dead, in order that we might bear fruit for God." (Romans 7:4)*

In writing to the Colossians Paul is making clear these three things:

- The Mosaic Law is a shadow that gives way to the reality of Jesus.

- The Sacrifices of the Mosaic Law gives way to the sacrifice of Jesus.

- The authority of the Mosaic Law gives way to the authority of Jesus.

*Colossians 2:18*

*"Let no one keep defrauding you of your prize by delighting in self-abasement and the worship of the angels, taking his stand on visions he has seen, inflated without cause by his fleshly mind."*

Again, the English here does not do justice to the inspired thoughts of Paul. The idea of being defrauded used by Paul here refers to the Greek or Roman games. The runner would be awarded a wreath on his victory, but he could lose the victory wreath if he was not careful in how he ran the race. If he listened to the wrong advice or accepted the wrong coaching, he would lose out. The idea of an athlete today being advised to take drugs to help him in the race comes to mind. He may think he has obtained his victory medal, but when he is tested and found to have run illegally, he will lose everything. Paul wrote to the Corinthians:

*"Do you not know that those who run in a race all run, but only one receives the prize? Run in such a way that you may win." (1 Corinthians 9:24)*

There is only one way to run the Christian race and that is by faith (See Hebrews 11-12) not works of the Law, as was being advised by the Colossian heretics. Paul then refers to how these deceivers work. The Greek underlying the text is speaking of an attitude that was adopted by those trying to defraud the Colossians. They took on the appearance of humility. In their seeking to seduce the Colossians, they would come across as sincere humble people. Paul had made reference earlier in verse 4 to them. They gave the appearance that they had the interests of the Colossians at heart but their intentions were evil. Indeed, as stated earlier, they were in the appearance of ministers of light, but came from the darkness. Their deception was the more dangerous because of this.

This explains Paul's reference in 2 Corinthians 11.14-15 The heretics at Colossae held themselves as humble servants wanting to do the will of God, their view of angels placed them too high and held them with esteem, giving glory to them that rightly belonged to God. (We can do this with so many things or people, making them our idols).

They also deluded themselves into believing they were humble and serving God's purposes. This is how they presented themselves in their attempts to deceive. This deception was birthed in false visions, which in turn were blown up out of all proportion and used to give foundation to the false teachings. Jeremiah had vehemently prophesied against such things:

> *"Thus says the LORD of hosts, "Do not listen to the words of the prophets who are prophesying to you. They are leading you into futility; they speak a vision of their own imagination, not from the mouth of the LORD."*
> *(Jeremiah 23:16)*

The situation never changes; the enemy of our soul continues to engage in such deception right up to this very day.

The reference to worshipping angels needs to be seen in this context. Whilst there are some records of Jews in the Babylonian situation involving themselves in inappropriate attitudes to angels, it is unlikely that they worshipped them in the sense we might think. In this culture, angels were seen as humble beings that only wanted to serve the higher purposes of God, such as guarding His saints. The Psalmist refers to this:

> *"For He will give His angels charge concerning you, to guard you in all your ways."*
> *(Psalm 91:11)*

> *"Bless the LORD, you His angels, mighty in strength, who perform His word, obeying the voice of His word! (Psalm 103:20)*

As was noted in the introduction, Paul also may well be addressing the popular legend of the archangel Michael being implored to aid the church at a time of disaster. This was entirely a false deception. Even in the modern visible church, we see and hear men and women announce such things. Concepts of the mind and imagination that parade as 'words of the Lord'. The wise minister of the Lord Jesus, Paul, rightly states:

> *"Quench not the Spirit; despise not prophesyings; prove all things; hold fast that which is good" (1 Thes 5:19-21)*

In being cautious we do not want to ignore or quench the work of the Spirit of God but we do need to test what is brought to us and only hold fast to that which discernment tells us if from God Himself.

**Colossians 2:19**
**" and not holding fast to the head, from whom the entire body, being supplied and held together by the joints and ligaments, grows with a growth which is from God."**

That the heretics once belonged to the body of believers (note how this follows on from verse 17) is seen here in Paul's opening phrase. They had detached themselves from Jesus, who, as Paul has already outlined in the letter, is the head of all things. This was particularly the truth of the true

Church, or the invisible Church, that only God knows. The entire body of these believers is nourished and fed by Jesus. By separating from Him, the individual withers and dies spiritually. Such an individual becomes open to deception and lies that leads them astray. Paul's body analogy is expanded in 1 Corinthians 12, where the whole body is fitted together and works as a unity attached to the Head Christ Jesus. Every joint and ligament is carefully placed and has functions operating within the distributed gifts that are inspired of the Holy Spirit. One of these gifts is discernment, which is lost by the individual when detached from the body. Such were these people who had lost such discernment and now were trapped in a deception that caused them to lose their crown of victory. They were now engaged in trying to seduce others to their sorry condition. Note too, that the growth of the body was from God. As it is written elsewhere unless the Lord builds the house, those that labour, labour in vain (Psalm 127:1). Indeed, Jesus Himself said, that He would build the Church (Matthew 16:18). The deceivers at Colossae were attempting to build a man-made house, but such a house has no life or solid ground, because it is built apart from Jesus, the true cornerstone and foundation.

***Colossians 2:20***

***"If you have died with Christ to the elementary principles of the world, why, as if you were***

*living in the world, do you submit yourself to*
*decrees.*"

Paul again raises the matters of Colossians 2:8ff. He asks the pointed question. If they have repented of their sins, believed in Jesus and were baptised into His death, why would they live as if this had never happened? This is the fundamental challenge to every follower of Jesus. It asks the question as to the effectiveness of our confession of faith. Paul has spelt out eloquently the facts of faith. In identifying with the death of Christ, we no longer live to Law – we live to Christ. The rules and regulations of the Mosaic Law have no longer any force over us. Rather we now live to the Law of the Spirit, in Christ Jesus (Romans 8:2). It is not that we do not physically live in the world, we do, but we are not off it (John 17:14).

Perhaps we can illustrate this with the analogy of two kingdoms. In the first kingdom the citizens are ruled by law, which must be obeyed to the letter and cannot be breached in any way. They live under the shadow of death for any such breach. In the second kingdom the citizens have accepted the rule of the king who has made a way for the citizens to live, without the concerns to keep the law. They now live for the king and out of love for him, live to serve him and their fellow citizens. Their lives are lived in freedom from a preoccupation with law and death and they now live a life of fullness in the grace of the king. If you live in the latter kingdom, why then would you still live as if you were a citizen of the former kingdom? This is Paul's point.

**Colossians 2:21**
**"Such as do not handle, do not taste, do not touch!"**

The style of writing here in the Greek is written in such a way to give emphasis to how the heretics would dictate to others. In a string of prohibitions do not, do not, do not, Paul is making clear the imprisoning effect of such attitudes. These attitudes draw the person into a paranoid world of fear and removes the freedom of grace and life. These phrases refer mainly to foods and possibly prohibitions on marriage. The Jewish traditions had brought in many concerns about handling and eating various foods. The Essene's had very strict rules about even touching people and their ideas had affected some early followers of Jesus. There was also some who would forbid marriage and Paul writing to Timothy speaks of both food and marriage issues:

*"Men who forbid marriage and advocate abstaining from foods which God has created to be gratefully shared in by those who believe and know the truth." 1Timothy 4:3*

It is possible Paul has here in mind such men as were at Colossae. Paul was against anyone who would try to bring the children of God into bondage with any form of legalism.

*Colossians 2:22*
*"(which all refer to things destined to perish with use)--in accordance with the commandments and teachings of men?"*

In a parenthesis Paul notes that these things that are being magnified as important were in fact things that would one day perish and disappear. Jesus Himself taught that even marriage would one day be finished (Matthew 22:30). Indeed, we read that Jesus spoke of these things concerning food:

> *"Do you not understand that everything that goes into the mouth passes into the stomach, and is eliminated? "But the things that proceed out of the mouth come from the heart, and those defile the man." Matthew 15:17-18*

Paul is consistent with the teachings of Jesus that what matters is the Law written on the heart – the Law of the Spirit. The contrast here in Paul's writing is with that which were simply the commandments and teachings which were the product of man's imaginations. The Jewish tradition had thrown up a host of rules and regulations that had never been on God's heart. Jesus again had spoken of this when referring to Isaiah 29:13:

> *"But in vain do they worship me, Teaching as*
> *their doctrines and instructions and the*
> *commands and precepts of men" Matthew 15:9*

Paul was exposing the vanity of men who would raise themselves above God. This is why the true disciple of Jesus must be clear what the Scriptures really teach and not slavishly follow some teaching of a man, no matter how great his reputation might be. This was indeed what the Greek Jews in the synagogue of Berea did, when Paul and Silas preached. They went home and studied the Scriptures to see if what was taught was true. From this many were saved.

### Colossians 2:23

***"These are matters which have, to be sure, the appearance of wisdom in self-made religion and self-abasement and severe treatment of the body, but are of no value against fleshly indulgence."***

Paul is no fool. He knows that from an outward appearance these heretics looked very sincere. They looked very wise in their manner. Their appearance of being very religious; their humble demeanour and their abuse of their own bodies in the name of God, all seemed so convincing. Paul has earlier written of this in verse 18 of this chapter. These appearances were deceptive and indeed the practices vain – pointless. The things these men did had no effect on the temptations of the flesh; their man-made religion could not deliver them from the grip of the struggle with sin. As Paul had written elsewhere on this struggle:

> *"Wretched man that I am! Who will set me*
> *free from the body of this death? Thanks be to*
> *God through Jesus Christ our Lord! So then, on*
> *the one hand I myself with my mind am serving*
> *the law of God, but on the other, with my flesh*
> *the law of sin." Romans 7:24-25*

In this passage from Romans, Paul is again alluding to the struggle between the *yetzer tov* and *yetzer ra* – the good and bad inclination - within man, as understood by the Jews. The Jewish teaching was that the practice of *Torah* would deliver the person. However, Paul now understood that through Jesus Christ he had been delivered and now lived to Him. (See above) He was concerned to free his readers from the idea of self-effort that negated the grace of God. Those in Colossae who had so been delivered by Christ were not now to resort again to the deceptions of the heretics, no matter how attractive they made it seem.

# Chapter Three

*Colossians 3:1-2*

**"If then you were raised with Christ, search for those things, which are above, where Christ is, sitting at the right hand of God. Set your mind on things above, not on things on the earth."**

Chapter three is introduced with the word 'if' or 'therefore'. That is Paul is calling attention to all that has been written so far in his letter. In particular he is looking back at his arguments about baptism (2:12). In this the believer had become dead to the world and to the Mosaic Law. The old man has gone. A new life had come. The preoccupation of the believer was not to be with the things of this world or living by some external code written on stones.

Just as Jesus had been raised from the dead, so too, the believer had been raised to new life. That life was now with a different focus. In searching those things which are above, Paul is pointing the believer to realise that all that is done in this life is now done through a mind set on eternal things. The word Paul uses for seeking or searching is ,in the underlying language, meaning to meditate, to dwell on and think about the Scriptures. It has the idea of owning or possessing the thing sought by such Scriptural study. That is the believer has to make the eternal things part of his nature. These things are 'above'. This means that the believers' view of the world is not to be based on the transient things of this life. This life is passing away and there are eternal spiritual realities that must inform how salvation is worked out. This does not mean total inaction on earth. Rather it means that the believer is to do the 'good works, God has prepared in advance' (Ephesians 2:10) in the Spirit of Christ. These works are to be done from a spiritually renewed heart, not from a legal codex, as was being promoted by the heretics at Colossae.

Paul goes on to state that the looking above will also bring into view the Lord Jesus who sits in the heavenly throne-room, at the right hand of God. This refers to the work of Jesus. In His death and resurrection, the work of salvation was completed. As was discussed earlier (1:15), Jesus is the pre-eminence of all creation. The act of sitting down as in Hebrews 1:3 is the act of a High Priest who has finished the work of atonement. No one can add to or take away from this by self-effort. Jesus has completed the work and now intercedes for those who are His (Hebrews 7:25). The believer is spurred on, not by the earthly impulses, but by the inner knowledge of a higher calling. That calling is of faith and speaks to us of Abraham, who journeyed through life, seeking a city yet to come (Hebrews 11:8-19). He was justified before God by faith and the believer also, is justified by that same faith - the journey of life is by such faith and not through the keeping of a legal codex.

*Colossians 3:3*

*"For you died, and your life is hidden with Christ in God."*

Paul is probably referring back to what he had written earlier (Colossians 2:3) in addressing the heresy at Colossae. The treasures of God, wisdom and knowledge, were in Christ. Through baptism the believer had died to the world and was now included in the spirituality of Christ. The believer's life was now secure and needed no further 'secret knowledge' offered by the heretics. Neither did the believer need to adhere to legal codices or rules but was to live according to the wisdom of the Spirit of Christ. Paul wrote to the Romans, that the law of the Spirit of life in Christ Jesus had set the believer free from the law of sin and of death. Indeed, Paul's great confession was proclaimed against those who would try to bind believers in legalism:

*"I have been crucified with Christ; and it is*
*no longer I who live, but Christ lives in me; and*
*the life which I now live in the flesh I live by faith*
*in the Son of God, who loved me and gave*
*Himself up for me." (Galatians 2:20)*

The Colossians' lives were 'hidden in Christ'. Even more securely their lives were 'hidden in Christ in God'. Grace had been shown to them and the merit of Christ was sufficient to secure their place in the eternity with God. They were freemen, and they were to hold on to their freedom and not be snared by the heresy that would suggest otherwise.

*Colossians 3:4*
*"When Christ He who is our life, now unseen*
*is manifested, then you also will be manifested*
*with Him in glory."*

It is this truth that Paul holds that calls him to remember his eternal destiny. It is no longer the believer, who lives, but their life is Christ and therefore that which has been committed to Him, He will keep until the day of His return (2 Timothy 1:12). It is on that day Paul, from his earliest days, believed that Christ would return with all His saints (1 Thessalonians 4:16-17). In a contrast to the previous verse, the believer who is now hidden in Christ will on the last day be revealed to the world, with Christ. Paul has run a thread throughout the letter of the true place of the believer. As noted above the believer has been raised up with Jesus, and we are 'hidden' in Him and He has seated us with Him in the heavenly places. It is when the close of earthly time comes, that this hidden state becomes a reality, as the natural body is gone and the new believer's spiritual body is made visible to all. We can have great joy in this and heed the words of Peter:

> *"But rejoice, in that as you are partakers of*
> *Christ's sufferings, when with His glory is*

*revealed, you may rejoice also with exceeding*

*joy" (1 Peter 4:13)*

In Colossians here, Paul again is addressing the heresy, wherein which the heretics offered a 'secret society', with the knowledge of salvation. Paul makes clear that the Messiah on His return will expose the lies and the true believers will be seen in all the glory of the Lord Jesus Christ. This is a great fillip to faith that holds to justification by faith alone, in the work of Christ. Knowing that one day we will see Him face to face, being unable to offer anything of our own effort to justify our being revealed with Him. The great hymn comes to mind:

Rock of Ages, cleft for me,

Let me hide myself in Thee;

Let the water and the blood,

From Thy wounded side which flowed,

Be of sin the double cure;

Save from wrath and make me pure.

Not the labour of my hands

Can fulfil Thy law's demands;

Could my zeal no respite know,

Could my tears forever flow,

All for sin could not atone;

Thou must save, and Thou alone.

Nothing in my hand I bring,

Simply to the cross I cling;

Naked, come to Thee for dress;

Helpless look to Thee for grace;

Foul, I to the fountain fly;

Wash me, Saviour, or I die.

While I draw this fleeting breath,

When mine eyes shall close in death,

When I soar to worlds unknown,

See Thee on Thy judgment throne,

Rock of Ages, cleft for me,

Let me hide myself in Thee.

(Augustus Montague Toplady, 1776)

*Colossians 3:5*

*"Therefore, put to death. the members of your body that you have on earth, as dead to immorality, impurity, passion, evil desire, and greed, which in effect is worshipping idols."*

Having laid out his understanding of the theology of being a believer in Christ and the truth of the believer being dead to the world, Paul sets out practical pastoral advice on how the believer is to live in the world. For Paul theology and doctrine of behaviour are inseparable, they are eternally entwined. The belonging to, and being in, Jesus, had to be 'worked out in fear and trembling' (Phil 2:12) (The Greek is in the plural, the body of Christ are to work salvation out together).

In this Paul is pointing to the natural body of desires, that should be put to death in baptism. The entering into baptism and the death and resurrection of the sinner into Christ, whilst real, must now be put into effect in the daily living of the believer in the communion of the saints. The believer is to reckon himself dead to the sins of the flesh. There is care needed here, as some have taken Paul's instructions (as in the KJV translation – 'mortify therefore your members') to mean self-flagellation and denial of pleasure for its own sake. This was never the idea of Paul. The sense of Paul's teaching is of concern for the 'other' in the community, not the 'self'. That is to say, the believer is now dead to his or her own self-centred desires and must now seek the rule and concern of Christ. Out of this love of Christ must flow a love for neighbour and enemy. Any selfish desires, which arise from the pursuit of selfish pleasure, must be put to death. Hence immorality, the entertaining of impurity of thought or deed, self-centred passion, the constant desire to do evil or the greed that seeks its own, is tantamount to one thing – idolatry - the worship of self rather than God in Christ. The rabbinic Paul maintains the truth of the Word of God: "You shall have no other gods before me" (Exodus 20:3).

*Colossians 3:6*

*"For it is because of this idolatry, that the wrath of God will come upon the sons of disobedience,"*

There is dispute about the phrase 'sons of disobedience' as this does not appear in the earliest manuscripts, but this does not take away from the intensity of Paul's inspired writing. Paul may have in mind a similar situation that was at Ephesus, when he wrote to them: "Do not be deceived by empty words, it is because of these things the wrath of God comes upon the sons of disobedience" (Eph 5:6). The empty words were here in Colossae, when the heretics preached the rejection of the Gospel Paul had preached. Their drawing away men to believe in self-effort and away from Jesus who turns God's wrath away from us, was a gross act of rebellion against God. It was the focus on the self as able to have the power that can only come from God, that turned the self into an idol. Paul is still so relevant to today, when we see so many being deluded by Social Media, to try and create their own perfection.

Whilst it is right to stress the great grace and mercy of God, as Paul does in other places, the full picture of God is only fully appreciated when there is the inclusion of God's wrath. Bearing in mind the heresy that was being taught by some at Colossae, There is an echo here of the Greek philosophy that saw the body separate from the soul, in which the body could be involved in evil acts but the soul still stays pure. Paul is consistent in his teaching which he also instructs the Romans: For the wrath of God is revealed from heaven against all ungodliness and unrighteousness of men, who by their unrighteousness suppress the truth" (Rom 1:18).

Those who taught another gospel, which was no Gospel, would no doubt be included in Paul's condemnation. He makes his readers aware that such disobedience, which is ultimately the rejection of Jesus, would expose the rebellious to God's ultimate wrath. As the well-known teacher David Pawson has commented, God puts justice before the love of people, and His wrath remains on those rebellious who have rejected God's grace and mercy.

In dealing with God's wrath it is important to point out that this is not a vindictive quality of God – one in which there is a spiteful anger. The rendering of 'wrath' here in Colossians requires clarification. The Greek word used in the Septuagint is more to do with disaster overtaking a person or group or of 'terrible judgements'. This gives a truer picture of the Jewish Paul's meaning. Those who decide to walk in evil ways will bring disaster on themselves and the judgement of God will come. The wrath of God is not vindictive but the just response to a choice by an individual.

**Colossians 3:7**
**"and in them you also once walked, when you were living in them"**

Paul no doubt has in mind the same idea that was also made clear to the Ephesians:

> *"And you who were made alive, were*
> *once dead in the stumbling and sins in*
> *which you once walked, following the*
> *course of this natural world, after the*
> *prince of the power of the air, the spirit that*
> *is now at work in the sons of disobedience"*
> *(Eph 2:1-2).*

Again, the Rabbinic Paul has in mind the Hebrew thought of *halakah* - that is the way a person should walk, according to the principles of *Torah*. This was not the legalism of the Law but following the guidelines of God's revealed word as the term *Torah* actually means. Paul's readers formally had a lifestyle that was alien to these principles. That walk caused them to stumble and fall from God's standards. Their walk was a walk of death that could have only one end – judgement and God's wrath as already discussed above. They had formerly lived in a way that had separated them from God and Paul is now reminding them of their condition before they had accepted Christ who had made reconciliation with God possible. Echoed here is Paul's writing to the Romans:

> *"Even so consider yourselves to be dead*
> *to sin, but alive to God in Christ Jesus"*
> *(Romans 6:11).*

Baptism had brought them to the death of self. They now lived in Christ and they must not forget their divesting of all that was of the world with its passions and their putting on Christ. Paul's reminder is to encourage them not to forget where they had come from, in order that they may not be stumbled in the race for the crown of victory (1 Cor 9:24-27), by the heretics at Colossae.

*Colossians 3:8*

*"But now you also, put of your mouth: anger, wrath, malice, slander, and abusive speech"*

In Judaism the tongue has the possibility of great harm. This was recognised in the *Torah*:

"You shall not go about as aa scandal monger
and talebearer, among your people, and you are
not to act against the life of your neighbour; I am
Yahweh" (Lev 19:16 ).

Yahweh, the one who was is and will be, was life giving. The idea in Judaism from this principle is *lashon ha-ra* – the evil tongue. The things Paul lists in this verse reflect this evil. The abusive speech that poured out from a person came from the heart (Matt 12:34). Judaism traditionally saw such speech as worse than theft and akin to murder. The prophet Jeremiah wrote of the wicked:

> *"Their tongue speaks out as a deadly*
> *arrow; it speaks deceit; with his mouth a*
> *person speaks of peace to his neighbour,*
> *but in his heart he lays an ambush for him.*
> *(Jer 9:8).*

Paul is direct in his instructions to believers that they are to be active in putting away these things: anger, wrath, malice, slander which were all abusive and destructive. Unlike theft, were restitution could be made, a person's character, when destroyed, was almost impossible to restore. I am minded of a Jewish story, wherein a man speaks evil of another and destroys his character. Coming to see he was wrong, the slander returned to the man and apologised and asked what could be done to undo the damage. The man gave him a bag of feathers and told him to go out and cast the feathers into the wind. Having scattered the feathers into the wind and seen them carried away over the land, he returned to the wronged man who then told him to go and gather up *all* the feathers again. The story makes the point well. James also makes clear the dangers of the tongue (James 3) and it behoves those who follow Christ to control the tongue and speak only that which is edifying. Furthermore, Paul also points out the idea of hypocrisy in which a person can speak to another warm words of peace but in their heart they are bitter and seeking a way to damage their neighbour. The believer needs to be aware that God is not ignorant of such deceit. God knows both the heart and the actions and He will judge accordingly. This is why Jeremiah speaks on the matter:

> *" The heart is polluted and deceitful above all things, and it is exceedingly corrupt: who can know it? I, Yahweh, search the mind, I try the heart, even to give every man according to his ways, according to the fruit of his doings" (Jer 17:9-10)*

### Colossians 3:9
**"Do not lie to one another, since you laid aside the old self with its evil practices"**

There is another echo here of *Halakah* with Paul using a clothing analogy. The old self was to be laid aside like a garment. This 'garment' was polluted, because it was a mixture of what God intended (purity) and sin (filth). Deuteronomy 22:11 and Leviticus 19:19 forbid the Jew wearing this man-made mixture. Wool was as God created it from the animal and linen was as God had created it from the plant, but in weaving them together, the resulting cloth was 'man-made'.

It is this idea of earthly contamination of man's Adamic nature by his actions that Paul teaches must be laid aside and the new uncontaminated nature of the second Adam must be put on.

Paul continues to refer to the evil tongue that speaks lies. It is from the contaminated nature at man's heart from which the mouth speaks,

> *"The good man out of the good treasure*
> *of his heart brings forth that which is good;*
> *and the evil man out of the evil treasure*
> *brings forth that which is evil; for his mouth*
> *speaks from that which fills his heart."*
> *(Luke 6:45)*

He begins to point to the creation of Adam. Satan deceived Adam and there is strong resonance of Paul's thoughts with the words of Jesus;

> *"You are of your father the devil, and*
> *you want to do the desires of your father.*
> *He was a murderer from the beginning and*
> *does not stand in the truth because there is*
> *no truth in him. Whenever he speaks a lie,*
> *he speaks from his own nature, for he is a*
> *liar and the father of lies. (John 8:44)*

In Adam's fall, the nature of man became diseased. It had a tendency towards the nature of the deceiver, which was that of a liar. This nature should never be of those in the community of Christ the new Adam. Paul wrote to the Ephesians,

> *"stop telling lies, speak only the truth*
> *each person with their neighbour, because*
> *we are all members of one body" (Eph 4:25).*

As members of the body of Christ, they were to relate in truth and love. Paul goes on to connect this with baptism. The candidate for baptism had removed his garments and laid them aside to be immersed into life with Christ. The follower of Jesus must 'lay aside the deeds of darkness' (Romans 13:12) and 'put on Christ' (Romans 13:14). There is little doubt that Paul has in mind his instructions given in Romans 6, where he reminds his readers that they have been crucified with Christ. The fleshly Adam with all his sinful nature was dead and the new Adam (Jesus) was the Christian's life. It is to this Paul points in the next verse.

***Colossians 3:10***
***"and have put on the new self who is being renewed to a true knowledge according to the image of the One who created him"***

The putting on of the new self is also found in Ephesians,

"..and put on the new self, which in the likeness of God has been created in righteousness and holiness of the truth" (Eph 4:24).

Both verses appear to refer to Genesis. Paul reminds the reader of the Creator God who made Adam in the perfection of the garden. God had always meant Adam to be pure and innocent and in loving relationship to Himself. The fall of Adam had fractured the image of God in man'

The human nature was now beset with a tendency towards evil practices that separated man from God.

In salvation the old was to be put off and the new put on. The new self was the work of Jesus, the new Adam, who was perfection and He had come to undo the work of sin that separated man from God. Paul had earlier referred to 'the true knowledge of God's Mystery, that is, Christ Himself' (2:2). It is this knowledge that they, and all Christians, were to grow in as they are renewed into the perfection of holiness. That is why salvation is a process of saved, being saved and ultimately saved into glory. The follower of Jesus is to lay aside all that would encumber them.

> "Therefore, since we have so great a cloud of witnesses surrounding us, let us also lay aside every encumbrance and the sin which so easily entangles us, and let us run with endurance the race that is set before us, fixing our eyes on Jesus, the author and perfecter of faith, who for the joy set before Him endured the cross, despising the shame, and has sat down at the right hand of the throne of God."
> (Hebrews 12:1-2)

This view in Hebrews is of the Messiah at the centre of the believer's universe. It lifts the believer out of a focus on the natural world onto the supernatural world (See 3:1:2 above) so that they continually grow, into the perfect image of God. There is a clear contrasting in Paul's mind: The fleshly Adam with its corrupt nature and the Messiah with His incorruptible nature and the first Adam in *the likeness of God* and the Messiah who was *the exact image of God*. Furthermore, Paul also has an eye to that glorious final transformation of the believer,

> "As is the earthy, so also are those who
> are earthy; and as is the heavenly, so also
> are those who are heavenly. Just as we
> have borne the image of the earthy, we
> will also bear the image of the heavenly."
> (1 Corinthians 15:48-49)

In the process of salvation, the movement of the disciple of Christ was away from the first (natural) Adam towards the second (supernatural) Adam in an active renewal to which Paul now turns.

### *Colossians 3:11*

*"..and in Him there is not Greek and Jew, circumcised and uncircumcised, barbarian, Scythian, slave and freeman, but in the Messiah is all, and in all"*

Carrying on from the previous verse, the thrust of the Greek here is that there is ONE Messiah and in Him all are one. It is a continuing renewing that speaks of quality of salvation. All, from any background, are saved by grace through faith equally – there are no degrees of salvation.

The renewal of the follower of Jesus not only involves a changing of mind but an active participation in putting off the old self. Paul puts the renewal in a current context to drive home his point. In a climate of heresy, where the heretics would seek to create an elite and an inferior that sows discord between members of the community, Paul points to the cosmic Christ. He highlights areas where there should be no division in the body of Christ. The Greek, or Gentiles to be specific, had no longer a dividing wall between them and the Jew. It had been torn down by Jesus' work (Eph 2:14-17). Paul underlines the point by the emphasis that the circumcised (the Jew) and the uncircumcised (the Gentile) have also no distinction, again echoed in Ephesians 2. This was also Paul's great argument to the Galatians,

"For neither is circumcision anything,

nor uncircumcision, but a new creation"

(Gal 6:15)

The new creation had no barriers between its members. It is important to note that here, and in Galatians 3:28, Paul is not doing away with race, nationality, or cultural differences. These continued. Gentiles were still Gentiles, Jews still Jews etc. etc. However, Jesus was "*kai en pāsin*" – all in everything. The Jew, the Greek, the Barbarian, Scythian, slave or freeman when covered by faith in Christ died and became incorporated into the new man,

*"Therefore, remember that formerly you, the Gentiles in the flesh, who are called "Uncircumcision" by the so-called "Circumcision," which is performed in the flesh by human hands. Remember that you were at that time separate from Christ, excluded from the commonwealth of Israel, and strangers to the covenants of promise, having no hope and without God in the world. But now in Christ Jesus you who formerly were far off have been brought near by the blood of Christ. For He Himself is our peace, who made both groups into one and broke down the barrier of the dividing wall, by abolishing in His flesh the enmity, which is the Law of commandments contained in ordinances, so that in Himself He might make the two into one new man, thus establishing peace" Ephesians 2:11-15*

Paul is stressing that in terms of salvation and incorporation into the cosmic Christ, there were no distinctions. The Colossian heresy that would divide was a false doctrine as is any idea that would suggest there is any hierarchy within the body of Christ. There is but one Royal

Priesthood, in which each renewed believer is called, according to the grace of God, to serve – each in their own calling.

*Colossians 3:12*
*"Therefore then, because you are chosen ones of God, holy ones and most beloved, have attitudes of compassion, pity graciousness, humility, gentleness, long-suffering.."*

Paul addresses those who have been brought into the New Man – the body of Christ. They are the elect they join the chosen of God. In addressing both Jews and Gentiles in the Colossian community, he is using a term that is familiar to Jews. They had always been the elect of God, but now the Gentiles had been grafted into the olive tree of Israel (Romans 11:17ff). For Paul the Jews had not been replaced by the Gentiles but the two had now become one. The Colossian heresy which would attempt to sow division and elitism was rejected. The New Man, including both Jew and Gentile, were holy and beloved. That is, set aside by the choice of the loving creator God. This choice called them to put on the new self as above in verse 10, but here Paul elaborates with the idea of a new heart.

For Paul the Jew, this reverberates with the promises in Ezekiel, where God promises a renewing work, that changes the heart of stone to a tender heart (Ezek 11:19, 36:26). Paul highlights certain qualities of this tender heart, beginning with compassion. In this the Colossians, indeed all followers of Jesus, are to be merciful to one another, showing pity and care, one to another without distinction. In his use of kindness, Paul would have the Hebrew words in mind that spoke of doing the greatest good in that spirit of mercy. Instead of arrogance or haughtiness reflected in the heretic's attitudes, they were to act in humility. These three attributes have strong echo of Micah, which encouraged the people of God, to know what God required of them,

> *"to do justly, love mercy and walk humbly*
> *before God" Micah 6:8*

This would require a gentle and patient attitude of mind that would bear with one another. To which Paul now turns.

> **Colossians 3:13**
> **"..bearing with one another, and forgiving each**
> **other, whoever has a complaint against anyone;**
> **just as the Lord forgave you, so also should**
> **you"**

In bearing with one another, there has to be forgiveness for wrongs suffered. Paul recognises that in every community, complaints or quarrels will arise. However, in this new community of Christ these things should not divide. They were to settle arguments quickly and to be reconciled through forgiveness. Paul again points them to Christ. Had *not the Lord the right to condemn and reject them, when they lived in* the old state of sin? Had He not been patient and kind to them, putting aside their transgressions and not holding it against them? Paul's teacher Gamaliel had taught *"So long as you are merciful, God will have mercy on you"*. It was a long-standing tradition in Judaism that a person must make peace before praying to God. Indeed, Jesus Himself often spoke of forgiveness as essential in any relationship with God. It is very striking that when Jesus tells the parable of the unforgiving servant, it is after the parable finishes He adds His own words,

> *"My heavenly Father will also do the* 
> *same to you (not forgive and punish), if each* 
> *of you does not forgive his brother from your* 
> *heart" (Matt 18:35).*

There is also the question as to the one being forgiven. Do they need to say 'sorry' or show repentance before being forgiven? Read the account of Zacchaeus. It is the presence of Jesus that caused Zacchaeus to change. There is no statement of saying 'sorry'. Zacchaeus, is so overwhelmed with the grace of Jesus, he is immediately transformed and wants to make amends. Then we look at the woman caught in adultery. The context of this encounter is very important in this subject of forgiveness. In the Temple at that time there was a service in progress that was just ending. The service was one of seeking forgiveness by the older men. The service contained this: 'The Chassidim and Men of Deed, "Oh joy, that our youth, devoted, sage, Doth bring no shame upon our old age!" The Penitents reply. "Oh joy, we can in our old age repair the sins of youth not sage!'". Both in unison. "Yes, happy he on whom no early guilt doth rest, And he who, having sinned, is now with pardon blest"". They would be streaming from this service and have seen the woman before Jesus. When Jesus makes the challenge for the one without sin to cast the first stone, who leaves first?

*"But when they heard it, they went away*
*one by one, beginning with the older ones,*
*and Jesus was left alone with the woman*
*standing before him".*

These older men had just experienced the forgiveness of God, they knew they had to walk away. Finally, note the woman does not say 'sorry'. Jesus' word to her was, "Neither do I condemn you; go, and from now on sin no more". His charge to her is to sin no more and she leaves forgiven and un-condemned.

Too often, our refusal to forgive can be fuelled with the notion that the other party has control over your willingness to forgive. They do not. You can be merciful and forgiving no matter what they do.

Paul expected the Colossians to follow their Saviour, who had demonstrated the perfect forgiveness as He suffered to purchase their salvation. In the throes of death He prayed, "Father forgive them...", In forgiving His enemies, Jesus speaks loudly, that there can never be un-forgiveness among the unified body of Christ.

*Colossians 3:14*

*"Beyond all these things put on love, which is*
*the perfect bond of unity."*

Having told the Colossians to *"put on a heart of compassion,*
*kindness, humility, gentleness and patience"*, Paul encourages them to
put love on over all these things. The Jewish Paul would know that love
covers a multitude of sins (Proverbs 10:12). The Hebrew *kâphar* has the
same meaning, to cover. For God so loved the world He had given His
only Son up to death to deal with sin and cover it and remove it.

This follows on from forgiveness, in which once forgiven, the sins
are covered and removed from sight. This is the act of love that reflects
the love of Jesus who made propitiation for our sins. That is the sins that
are removed and covered are ultimately dealt with by Jesus, in that He
took them on Himself and satisfied the demands of justice. Once this
was done we were freed from any demands of justice and can never be
anymore condemned or accused. It is beautifully said through the
prophet Micah,

> "He will again have compassion on us; He
> will tread our iniquities under foot. Yes, You
> will cast all their sins into the depths of the
> sea" (Mic 7:19)

Who can fail to call to mind Paul's great anthem of love in 1
Corinthians 13? There Paul is speaking of the unity of the body, whose

spiritual unity is rooted in love. Here Paul's imagery speaks of the clothing being put on and above them all is the outer garment of love that others will see. This garment is held also is a means of binding all the graces together into a unity. The truer rendering would suggest that the bond is one of perfection. Such is the true love of Christ, that perfect love that we are to live. It is such love that will hold the community of grace together. Through the selfless compassion, kindness, humility, gentleness, held together in love, it will be demonstrated to a needy world, that the community belongs to Jesus and are His disciples.

**Colossians 3:15**
**"Let the peace of Christ rule in your hearts, to which indeed you were called in one body; and be thankful."**

Wherever there are disputes and arguments, disagreements or divisions, there is a need for an arbitrator or referee. Jesus had taught in Matthew 18 the means of resolution of such things through the community of God. Paul himself rebuked the Corinthians for going outside the community for judges to decide between them (1 Cor 6).

Here Paul calls for the peace of Christ to 'rule' or better 'arbitrate'. It is also good to go back to the language source from which Paul's idea of peace comes. That is *shalom*. Touched on previously, *shalom* it is not merely 'peace' that is one meaning, but it is a complete wholeness or unity of wellbeing. It is the sense of welfare and the absence of war and strife. Christ had turned away from the community the hostility of God against sin. He had brought the *shalom* of God into the world and was the arbitrator between them and God. He brought eternal peace.

In the heart of the Colossians, Paul is calling for this attitude of *shalom* of the Messiah to be the arbitrator in their disputes. The Church, the called-out community, had been called to such *shalom*. Earlier (Chapter 2:14) Paul had reminded them of what God had done in causing the hostile decrees to be removed. They had been called to *shalom*. Now the community was also to ensure that this *shalom* reigned in their hearts and community. Not only this, they should be thankful. If they truly understood what God had done in causing His anger to cease against them, then thanks would pour from them. He no longer held their sins against them - this should cause them to be ever grateful. In that gratitude they would hold the right attitudes one to another. Many times the Psalmist sings:

"Give thanks unto Yahweh; for He is rich
in goodness; For his lovingkindness is never-
ending" (Psalm 136:1)

May this eve be our song to the great and wonderful Father who gave us His Son and with grateful hearts love others as He has loved us!

*Colossians 3:16*

*"Let the word of Christ richly dwell within you,*
*with all wisdom teaching and admonishing one*
*another with psalms and hymns and spiritual*
*songs, singing with thankfulness in your hearts*
*to God."*

Here we find, the only place in Scripture, the phrase *"the word of the Christ"*. In Romans 10:17, Paul writes, *'So then faith comes by hearing, and hearing by the word of God'*. Some translations interpret this as the Word of Christ. This is an interpretation that concludes the Word of God is and is about the Christ. In Colossians, there are two possible genitives in the Greek, which can render the term as the word delivered by Christ or the word about Christ. In the context of the letter, Paul has been going to great pains to show the cosmic Christ and His work. It would seem appropriate that Paul would mean 'the word about Christ' here.

It is Paul's word about Christ that has made clear Christ's work in redemption and freedom from sin and death for them. Paul has sown in his word about Christ how He is the centre of everything. Paul has encouraged the Colossians to follow the example of Christ (cf 3:13). It is these truths about Christ that Paul has outlined that should dwell within them. Again, Paul is using a term to indicate that the word about Christ should 'live with them' or 'make a home with them'. Not only this, but it should be found 'richly' or 'abundantly' with them. There is to be no meanness in the fullness of their knowledge of Christ. It is to live with them continually to inform them, as they act on Paul's teaching and in their dealing with the heretics and that corrupt teaching they were bringing.

Paul also encourages them to act in all wisdom - not earthly wisdom or the heretical wisdom being preached, but the wisdom that is the fruit of the Spirit. This is what Paul had written at the beginning of this letter (1:9). It is in that knowledge of Christ they are to 'teach' and 'admonish' one another. By implication the teaching has to be in line with Paul's teaching and to ensure no one is misled by the heretics. Secondly, where necessary they are to 'admonish' one another. Paul had given similar instructions to the Thessalonians, indicating that such admonishment should be 'as a brother'. As discussed earlier, the word used, '*noutheteō*' carries this idea, in that the reproof, or warning given, must be gentle. This reflects again the way Christ had dealt with them.

Paul suggests that some ways this might be achieved is in their gatherings, using the Psalms from the wisdom literature of the *Tanach*. There were also the hymns that were emerging among the redeemed community. Paul himself had in this letter penned a hymn to the cosmic Christ, which would remind the hearers of the great work of Christ (1:15-22). The use of these is collected in Pauls term 'spiritual songs'. That is, the singing of the community should be inspired by the Spirit and not the flesh. Such spiritual singing will bring the teaching and gentle warnings that will ensure the community stay focused on Christ and not stray into personal fleshly spite or jealousy. Hence Paul's 'with grace' which is a better rendering of '*charis*'. This is the same grace that Christ had shown them. At this point Paul states this is a matter of the heart, not simply lip service. The hearts of the Colossians need to be centred on the Lord, and in their relationship to one another He must rule. Paul moves to underline this in the next verse.

*Colossians 3:17*
*"Whatever you do in word or deed, do all in the name of the Lord Jesus, giving thanks through Him to God the Father."*

There is to be no exception in how the Colossians should behave, it is every word or deed, in civil or spiritual activity that is to be done, *'in the name of the Lord Jesus'*. The phraseology is, as always, not accidental. Again, we find the Hebrew thought of '*shem*' (Hebrew for 'name') that would be with Paul, is not simply a label that a person has. It embraces the whole nature and character of the person. The words and deeds are to be in that nature and character of Christ. Paul has ably outlined how salvation was brought about by Christ, through grace and mercy. That is the nature and character Paul has urged the Colossians to embrace. In other places it is 'in the name of the Lord' or *'in the name of God'*. The point is the same, the nature and character of God, the

Lord, the Messiah, have been revealed by the Spirit to believers. Paul's understanding is clear in a reference to the cosmic Christ in Ephesians:

*"In Him we have redemption through His blood, the forgiveness of our trespasses, according to the riches of His grace which He lavished on us. In all wisdom and insight, He made known to us the mystery of His will, according to His kind intention which He purposed in Him with a view to an administration suitable to the fullness of the times, that is, the summing up of all things in Christ, things in the heavens and things on the earth. In Him also we have obtained an inheritance, having been predestined according to His purpose who works all things after the counsel of His will, to the end that we who were the first to hope in Christ would be to the praise of His glory" Ephesians 1:7-12*

Paul expected all men, to behave in such a way that honoured the name of Christ and caused praise and glory to be given to Him. Again, Paul also returns to the theme of giving thanks with this being the fourth time he has encouraged an attitude of thankfulness. As commented earlier (1:12) the thankfulness relates to the joy of being 'qualified' or 'sufficient', because of Christ, to share in eternal life. If the believer fully grasps just how gracious God has been in Christ, then the only attitude is thanks, with a subsequent outpouring of grace and mercy towards others. As the Messiah taught, he who has been forgiven much loves much' (Luke 7:47). And it is through, or in the name of, this Christ the thanks are made. For He alone is the mediator who has brought us to the Father (1 Timothy 2:5); it is He who stands ever before the throne making intercession (Hebrew 7:5). It is He who has made us acceptable and it is fitting that it is through him all prayer and thanksgiving should be made.

### Colossians 3:18
### "Wives, be subject to your husbands, as is fitting in the Lord"

At the time of Paul's writing the practical instructions that would follow, were written in a very different age than today. The advice Paul brings is a Godly wisdom that would be against the trends of the society then. The situation in both Jewish and Greek culture had women, children and slaves in an inferior position. The wife was a chattel of the husband, the child a possession of the father who could even sell him, and the slave had no rights under law.

Paul however, expresses the heart of a loving gracious Father who insists on a mutual obligation in all relationships. Both the wife and the husband have responsibilities towards one and other in terms of respect and love. The child has to honour the parents and the parents to encourage and support the child. The slave is to serve willingly and dutifully, whilst the master is to be gracious and merciful to his slave.

Writing in the 21$^{st}$ century, with the events of the 'liberating 60's' and the women's liberation movement inspired by feminism, the Scripture here, as in other places, continues to go against societal trends for different reasons. However, the negative reaction to these verses is often through an ignorant understanding of them. As we will see the Spirit inspires Paul to set the subjection of wives in a context of love. Paul had made a larger statement on a wife's subjection in his letter to the Ephesians (Chapter 5).

Paul taught that the relationship between men and women was grounded in creation (I Timothy 2:13-14). The woman had been made to be the helpmate of the man, created first. This order of creation called the woman to acknowledge her relationship to her husband as one of submission and obedience. However, this obedience is to be as to the Lord (Eph 5:22) or as here 'fitting in the Lord', which requires the man to act towards his wife in the nature and character of Christ. In this way the submitting wife is acting in the manner Paul has been teaching in previous verses.

### Colossians 3:19
*"Husbands, love your wives and do not be embittered against them."*

Following from the previous verse, Paul instructs the husband in his responsibility. He stresses the context of the relationship of husband and wife is rooted love. Elsewhere Paul expresses his understanding that this love of the husband for his wife is to be as Christ loves the Church (Ephesians 5). Furthermore, there is the charge from Paul that the husband must not be embittered towards his wife. This verse demonstrates the fact that love and bitterness are opposites and opposed to one another. Where the fragrance of love is there is no room for bitterness, and where bitterness reigns then love will die and be absent. The embittered heart is a desperate thing as the Psalmist wrote:

*"When my heart was embittered And I was pierced within, Then I was senseless and ignorant; I was a beast before You"* Psalms 73:21-22

Such a beast is a husband who abandons love towards his wife and allows bitterness to take over.

***Colossians 3:20***
***"Children, be obedient to your parents in all things, for this is well-pleasing to the Lord."***

Paul continues in his practical instruction, turning to the children of the marriage union. Here he calls for obedience to parents. This study is written at a time when society has become 'child centred'. A time when national and international bodies have allowed laws to enable children to prosecute their parents and in one sad case, a child is allowed to 'divorce' himself from his parents. Although well-meaning, these things have moved from God's wisdom, here expressed by Paul.

As a Hebrew, Paul as a child would have begun at the age of five to learn the *Torah*, and its commands to honour parents. He would have been trained in these things and as a man he would not have departed from them. So, it is with children, they are to be trained in the way of the Lord (Deut 5) and are to be taught the great works of God. From this they are to develop responsibility and obedience to parents. Paul here does not appeal to law but refers to the fact that it is well pleasing to the Lord. Here we see that true obedience is a matter of heart not law. A heart that is after the Lord, is an obedient heart and needs no other force than the desire to please the Master.

### *Colossians 3:21*
*"Fathers, do not exasperate your children, so that they will not lose heart."*

The wise Paul knows that there is a relational context to obedience. His advice is to remind fathers, the heads of families, not to provoke their children to anger, as is the sense of the words. A child needs correction and discipline, but they also need encouragement. The Lord would have the same attitude in fathers that is in the heavenly Father, who so loved them that he provided the Messiah to die. Such love must govern the father and child relationship that a father would give up all in the love of his child. Such love should govern the father's heart, so that the child would grow and not lose heart or be discouraged.

**Colossians 3:22**
**"Slaves, in all things obey those who are your masters on earth, not with external service, as those who merely please men, but with sincerity of heart, fearing the Lord."**

At this time in human history, the idea of a slave today would be totally unacceptable, although it still goes on in some parts of the world. In Paul's day, slaves were commonplace, and their conditions could often be quite arduous. For the Jew, the treatment of slaves or servants was regulated by God's Word. This advocated a merciful and gracious oversight by the master. However, slavery was still slavery and the person's freedom and life were totally controlled by the master. For the slave Paul brings a spiritual understanding to being a slave. When he or she was purchased by the Messiah, they belonged to Him. Paul understands, expressed elsewhere (Rom 6:18), that this made all believers, slaves of righteousness. However, a slave in the earthly sense was a freedman of the Lord (1 Cor 7:22). That was, in spiritual terms, the believer must not be a slave to another man. In this then Paul could counsel that slaves were free to obey their masters on earth, being firstly subjected to Jesus.

As always in Paul's teaching, this would be understood as a matter of the heart that had been changed by the Messiah. The service was not just for external purpose, to look good, but it was as to please the Lord, the true Master. In that Paul sets the basis of his counsel is the 'fear of the Lord/God'. This is best understood in the context of 'reverence' or 'awe' for God. Because a Christian slave bears His name, any bad behaviour on the slave's part would bring slander to God's name.

Today, it is the same for those who are employed. At work the Christian is to have the same attitude towards those in authority over them. If a slave in Paul's time who received no 'wage' was so called, how much more those who receive a payment for their service?

*Colossians 3:23*

*"Whatever you do, do your work heartily as for the Lord rather than for men"*

Paul stresses by repetition that the slave's service, is to be 'out of' or 'from' the 'soul', as the language is. In switching from 'heart' in the previous verse, to 'soul' here, Paul is emphasising, as in Ephesians (Eph 6:7), that the service rendered is more than a mere token but is to be done with a true devotion. Why? Because the service rendered was not to men but was to the Lord. Paul himself, as a Hebrew, understood that the most God centred slave, would have that attitude in the *Torah*, demonstrated in Exodus 21:5, were out of love of his master, he, with his whole family, would rather remain in slavery than be free. Christ's own demonstration of this attitude, even in Himself, was that momentous cleaning of the feet of His own disciples (John 13).

**Colossians 3:24**
**"knowing that from the Lord you will receive the reward of the inheritance. It is the Lord Christ whom you serve."**

Paul now points the slave to a higher calling. The language suggests that Paul wants an opening of the eyes that brings discernment. The slave is not to look at his situation with earthly eyes but to see the future reward that is to come. That is the blessedness of the eternal abode, where they will spend eternity with their great heavenly Master who is the one they really serve. This was the inheritance of the saints Paul had referred to earlier in the letter (Col 1:12).

In using the term 'reward', Paul is addressing slaves in the language they would understand. He is not suggesting that the inheritance is something they will receive as a merit for their effort. The inheritance is a matter of grace. It is given to those who do not deserve it. As Paul wrote to the Ephesians; *"For by grace you have been saved through faith; and that not of yourselves, it is the gift of God; not as a result of works, so that no one may boast"* Ephesians 2:8-9). So, the slave is to serve in faith and grace, knowing that he or she is the undeserving object of love. It is in this knowledge we are all to serve our earthly authorities, with our eyes fixed on the Master, Christ, who is the author and finisher of the faith that sustains us through this life.

*Colossians 3:25*
*"For he who does wrong will receive the consequences of the wrong which he has done, and that without partiality."*

The language does not make clear if Paul is addressing slaves or all men, including masters. However, it is of no matter, the principle is universal in the economy of God. For the one who does wrong (and here it means, to offend, to hurt or to be unjust), has to bear in mind that there will be consequences. Paul turns the consequences on the word 'receive'.

Previously the dutiful servant would receive the good reward of the inheritance. However, the wrongdoer will receive the punishment for wrongdoing. This is the universal truth that must govern the behaviour of the believer. The child of God must be honest in his endeavour and whether master or slave, the treatment of others and the attention to duty, requires the highest standard of integrity. The abdication of this responsibility will bring consequences, possibly in this life and certainly in the world to come. As Paul wrote to the Romans:

*"We know that the judgment of God, according to righteousness, falls on those who practice such things. Do you really think, O man - you who judge those who practice such things and then you yourself go and do them - that you will escape the judgment of God? Or do you think you can take advantage of the riches of his kindness and forbearance and patience, not understanding that God's kindness is meant to lead you to repentance? But because of your hard and unrepentant heart you are storing up wrath for yourself on that day of wrath when God's righteous judgment will be revealed. He will render to each one according to his works: to those who by patience in well-doing seek for glory and honour and immortality, He will give the reward of eternal life; but for those who are self-seeking and do not obey the truth, but obey unrighteousness, there will be wrath and fury. There will be tribulation and distress for every human being who does evil, the Jew first and also the Greek" Romans 2:5-9*

In that judgement, Paul here in Colossians makes clear, that the Judge is without partiality. That is, justice is rendered in accordance with divine principles that have been made clear to man. No one will be able to claim exemption. As Paul makes clear in Romans, 'they are without excuse" (Romans 1:20).

# Chapter Four

*Colossians 4:1*

*"Masters, grant to your slaves justice and fairness, knowing that you too have a Master in heaven."*

As already noted, rom the 13<sup>th</sup> and 16<sup>th</sup> century onwards men began to divide the Scriptures into portions, with chapters and verses to ease referencing. However, here is a case in point where they got it wrong.

This verse clearly continues Paul's thoughts that were discussed above in chapter 3. As he had lifted the eyes of the slave to heaven in their service to earthly masters, Paul calls now to masters to do the same.

Firstly, Paul highlights justice and the resulting fairness. When their slaves had rendered service, the masters are duty bound to respond justly in terms of the slave's situation. The slave had a right to sustenance, clothes, accommodation, good working conditions. Not only was this the case, but the provision of such things was to be fair. Their treatment and oversight were not to be overbearing or harsh but was to be as that of the Heavenly Master, who as Paul had outlined in this letter was gracious and merciful towards them. Paul, as a Hebrew, would be well aware that the Lord had set out clearly how a slave should be dealt with (Exodus 21). If the legal requirements of the treatment of slaves were so merciful, how much more so, should a master who follows the

Messiah be just and fair with his slaves? Indeed, the care of a person's health and safety is not a modern idea, even God made it a priority,

> *"When you build a new house, you shall make a parapet for your roof, so that you will not bring bloodguilt on your house if anyone falls from it"*
> *Deuteronomy 22:8*

Just as the Scriptures speak to workers today, they also speak to employers of labour in terms of how they treat their workers. Both should be aware of their Master in Heaven who watches over all the activities of men.

### *Colossians 4:2*
### *"Devote yourselves to prayer, keeping alert in it with an attitude of thanksgiving;"*

Paul only uses this Greek word (*proskartereō* - here 'devote') three times in the letters ascribed to him, twice in connection with prayer. Paul has probably in mind the understanding of the Hebrew *chazaq*. That is to strengthen oneself or remain steadfast. The call of the Messiah was a call to a life of self-sacrifice. Paul had outlined some practical matters in which the Colossians were to follow the example of the One who had called them. These things would often require a response beyond the human will and self-interest. In this then, was the value of prayer to strengthen and encourage the believer. The focus of prayer being God in the Messiah would ever keep the believer's mind on the heavenly and keep him or her alert to the spiritual dimension of life.

In this attitude, the practical application of Paul's instructions would be more ably implemented. The follower of Christ today is no different to man throughout the ages. Everything in the world often seeks to draw the follower away from God and His Christ and to weaken faith. It is essential that prayer be a constant activity. Both the praise and worship in prayer, and the desperate cries of our struggles, all reach the Master, who in grace and mercy responds out of His great bounty.

As always Paul links prayer to an attitude of thanksgiving. He has demonstrated throughout the letter the majestic work of the cosmic Christ that brought to the undeserving, the magnificence of God's riches. With such grace and mercy then, is the believer to be grateful and to flavour all prayer with such thankfulness.

*Colossians 4:3*
*"praying at the same time for us as well, that*
*God will open up to us a door for the word, so*
*that we may speak forth the mystery of Christ,*
*for which I have also been imprisoned;"*

This verse in many ways demonstrates Paul's humiliation for the sake of the Gospel. Firstly, the great Apostle is not too proud to ask for prayer, for himself and Timothy. It is an arrogant and foolish preacher who seeks to move in ministry without praying people to support him. It is also a reminder that the people of God should be in constant prayer for those who preach the Word. The prayer that God will open a door for the proclamation of the Good News is to be combined with intercession for the preacher and the results of his preaching.

For Paul here, it was imprisonment and many other hardships (2 Cor 11:33). Indeed, Paul was aware that when a door opened for the Gospel, opponents were not far behind (1 Cor 16:9). Even though Paul rejoiced in his suffering, as he had written earlier, (Col 1:24) he needed the comfort of the knowledge that others were praying for him (Philippians 1:9). So all believers need to appreciate that praying for those who take the great mystery of the cosmic Christ to a fallen world, is an essential part of spreading the Gospel. It is what makes us all fellow labourers in the vineyard – the leader and the led.

### Colossians 4:4
*"that I may make it clear in the way I ought to speak."*

Here again is the humble Paul. There is a need to understand that Paul is highly educated and eloquent. His authority and labouring for the Gospel had brought great status among the Gentile churches, if not the Jerusalem church. In that then there is the possibility of arrogance and pride that could cause wrong motives in the preaching of the Word.

The Gospel is simple and plain, it is not a vehicle for anyone to demonstrate their intellect and cleverness or to play to the crowd for applause. Paul asks for prayer that he will be able to make the mystery of Christ clear and that his preaching will be spoken in the right manner. When Spurgeon was complimented on being a great preacher, he made clear he would rather people spoke of a great God, after he preached. This too is Paul's motive.

**Colossians 4:5**
**"As you walk through life, yourselves do so with wisdom toward outsiders, making the most of the opportunity."**

It is in this verse we find the Hebrew Paul, bringing together Hebrew and Greek thinking. Many translate the term here 'conduct', the Greek has 'walk'. Conduct however, does catch better the Hebrew thought of Paul, in that he again has in mind the Hebrew principle of *halakah*. He uses this a number of times in the letter. The principles of the believer's walk must be based on the example of the cosmic Christ – that is how a person should walk through life.

For the Jew this was through the *Torah*. However, here in Colossians, Paul has been building on the person and work of Christ as the pattern for the believer. He is the *Torah*, the Word of God made flesh. The believer is to conduct themselves towards outsiders in the knowledge that they represent this Cosmic Christ, the Lord of the universe. They are to do this with 'wisdom' (*Sophia*). This was not to be the wisdom of words (1 Cor 1:7) but their behaviour was to demonstrate the wisdom of God in Christ:

> *"But by His doing you are in Christ Jesus,*
> *who Himself became to us the wisdom from*
> *God, and righteousness and sanctification,*
> *and redemption," (1 Corinthians 1:30)*

The redeemed are to demonstrate righteousness and sanctification in their dealings with those outside the community of Christ. So often the words of Christians are not heard by unbelievers because their words are drowned out by their un-Godly behaviour.

Furthermore, Paul writes of ransoming the time, translated here as 'making the most of the opportunity'. It is clear Paul is not meaning the chronological time, minutes, hours, days, months etc. He uses *Kairos*, which is time, understood by events and moments of experience. The Sophists used the term to describe the taking of opportunity found in changing circumstances.

No doubt Paul is also is thinking of opportunities where the Gospel might be demonstrated in word and action. Rather than waste precious moments like these, they are to be redeemed, bought, for the sake of Christ. The use of *Kairos*, in Mark for example (Mark 1:15), speaks of the appointed times of God. Believers should be alert to the wisdom of the Spirit in divinely appointed moments of life, when God desires to break through into the lives of unbelievers.

**Colossians 4:6**
**"When you speak, always do so with grace, as**
**though seasoned with salt, so that you will know**
**how you should respond to each person."**

Paul now once more brings a concrete example of *halakah*. The Rabbinic Paul is concerned with the Hebraic *halakah* on the tongue - *Lashon Ha-Ra* – the evil tongue he has mentioned before. The Psalmist wrote,

> *"Keep thy tongue from evil, and thy lips from speaking guile" Psalm 34:13*

Scripture contains many references to the danger of the tongue (cf. James 3:6). Here Paul encourages the believer to speak with grace. What a beautiful thing is grace. The very Word of God, His speech, spoke to us in grace through the Messiah. It spoke to wretched sinners the good news of forgiveness and love.

It is that same undeserved grace that is to flavour our speech. Paul writes, 'as though seasoned with salt'. Everyone knows that a good meal is ruined if not properly salted. Indeed, the meal may contain the best of ingredients, but if not seasoned, it is inedible. The believer who seasons their speech with grace will be heard and received. In that then when anyone asks about the believer's faith in Christ, the reply so seasoned, will likely be heard.

> *Colossians 4:7-8*
> *"As to all my affairs, Tychicus, our beloved brother and faithful servant and fellow bond-servant in the Lord, will bring you information. For I have sent him to you for this very purpose, that you may know about our circumstances and that he may encourage your hearts;"*

Paul now turns to completing his letter and mentions many of the saints who laboured with him for the sake of Christ. Here he writes of Tychicus. This man was a travelling companion of Paul and with him in his imprisonment. He is an inspiration as one who has been transformed by the cosmic Christ. 'Beloved' and 'faithful', used here by Paul, speak of this man who was a willing and obedient bond servant. He had ministered under Paul's instructions in Asia, replacing Titus to allow him to travel to Paul.

This trusted man when free, was to reliably impart to the Colossians information from Paul. Indeed, this was the specific reason why Tychicus had been the carrier of this letter. Paul could rely on him to communicate effectively Paul's situation in prison. Not in a negative way but in such a way that the difficulties of Paul's situation could be demonstrated to be to the purposes and glory of Christ and an encouragement to the faithful. Such then is our example, that we as people carry the Word of God to the world and to believers; and to both we declare the encouragements of faith to all.

*Colossians 4:9*

*"and with him Onesimus, our faithful and beloved brother, who is one of your number. They will inform you about the whole situation here."*

This is a beautiful verse. Onesimus was a member of this community. In the past he had been useless (Philm 1:11) - a slave who had run away from his master Philemon – and a slave who had defrauded his master (Philm 1:18). But now changed by the work of Christ, he was also 'faithful' and 'beloved'. What transforming grace we see here, that reaches out from heaven and makes the useless, profitable, the worthless, precious. This slave, who ran from the service of an earthly master, was found by the heavenly Master and turned around to serve anew. Indeed, here he is commissioned by Paul as a worthy witness with Tychicus to confirm his situation and through the Word of God to testify to us that there is redemption for everyman, for every slave of sin.

*Colossians 4:10-11*

*"Aristarchus, my fellow prisoner, sends you his greetings; and also Barnabas's cousin Mark (about whom you received instructions; if he comes to you, welcome him); and also Jesus who is called Justus; these are the only fellow workers for the kingdom of God who are from the circumcision, and they have proved to be an encouragement to me."*

In these closing verses, the reader might pass over the Scripture too quickly and miss some encouragement from the Spirit. Mentioned are Aristarchus, Mark and Justus. Paul was the only one under arrest, yet Aristarchus had surrendered his own freedom to share Paul's captivity. This was the same man who was mobbed by the crowd when he was with Paul in Ephesus. Such is the character of a true convert to Christ, who would lay down his life for his brother in the Lord and who would suffer deprivation for the sake of the Gospel. Indeed, an example for us to follow.

Secondly Paul mentions Mark. Mark was the spiritual son of Peter and cousin to Barnabas. He had travelled before with Paul but had deserted Paul during a missionary journey. The result of this was a dispute between Barnabas and Paul, when Mark was rejected by Paul for a later mission (Acts 15:37-39). Too often Christians have differences of opinions and arguments that result in splits and divisions, which run on for years. But see here the Apostle Paul demonstrating that the matters have been resolved and the divided parties reunited for Christ's sake. No doubt word had got around of the dispute, so Paul makes clear that the past has gone and now Mark is to be welcomed as a fellow brother. This is a sign of true redemption and appreciation of grace, when healing of relationships is part of the Christian experience, and forgiveness releases all parties to continue to serve the Messiah.

Finally, Justus is mentioned. Although not certain, this is likely to be the one who gave shelter to Paul at Corinth (Acts 18:7). In a situation where Paul was rejected by the Jews for preaching Jesus as the Messiah, this man stood with him and gave him shelter. A worshipper of God he was not afraid to be associated with Paul for the sake of the Gospel. The challenge to the reader is the willingness to stand and be counted for the Gospels sake, when in difficult circumstances.

At the time of Paul writing the letter he states that these three were the only ones of the circumcision who worked with him in Rome. That is to say these were the only Jews who had accepted Jesus as their Messiah, who served with Paul in Rome. There were many such Jews there, but only these three would associate with Paul in the work of the Gospel to the Gentiles. Again, how easy it is to be a fair-weather Christian, but when the Spirit calls to service will the fear of an in-group, causing stumbling in the service of the Messiah? Paul honours them with the comment that they had been an encouragement to him in his trials and imprisonment in Rome. May we too be found to be people of encouragement to others who labour for Christ.

> *Colossians 4:12-13*
> *"Epaphras, who is one of your number, a bondslave of Jesus Christ, sends you his greetings, always labouring earnestly for you in his prayers, that you may stand perfect and fully assured in all the will of God. For I testify for him that he has a deep concern for you and for those who are in Laodicea and Hierapolis."*

In these closing verses we again see Paul mention Epaphras. The study has spoken in other places of this great servant of God. Paul reminds the Colossians that Epaphras is one of them. He adds that He is a bondservant of Christ. He had laboured for them when with them, teaching the Gospel and building them up in truth. Now having been sent to minister to Paul, he had become a fellow prisoner and labourer with Paul in Rome.

However, like any good Pastor, he had not forgotten his flock. He laboured earnestly for them in prayer. The sense of the Greek is a struggle, a wrestling. It is not too hard to understand why such a fierce activity in prayer. Epaphras would be well aware of the wolves at Colossae who would tempt the faithful away from Christ with their heresy. Words alone would not suffice in the battle. Spiritual warfare needs the constant waging of battle in the heavenly realm.

The Apostle Paul reveals the content of the prayer *'that you may stand perfect and fully assured in all the will of God'*. As we have seen in this study, the heretics had suggested that the work of the Cosmic Christ was not complete and required further works in order to be perfected. Their Pastor's prayer was that they would stand perfect [in Christ] and not be swayed by winds of false doctrine.

Furthermore, the prayer was for their full assurance in the will of God for them. The Greek is meaning that they would have an assurance in what God had willed for them. This of course was for their salvation in Christ by faith alone as Paul had so strongly argued throughout this letter. The agony of this prayerful Pastor, was seen and witnessed by Paul who could stand in testimony to Epaphras' concerns, not only for them but those believers in that area. Such Spirit inspired Scripture is written to all believers as a call to fervent prayer for all believers to stand perfect and fully assured of God's will for them.

### Colossians 4:14
*"Luke, the beloved physician, sends you his greetings, and also Demas."*

Again, we must pause to draw from the well of spiritual insight this small verse gives. Luke, the author of a Gospel and The Acts, that recorded the history of the emerging Church, is the sender of greetings. However, here he is not given a spiritual title or description, but his human profession of 'physician' or 'doctor'.

Why has the Spirit inspired this? Could it be that it is to correct the extreme activity of so-called faith healers, who see no room in healing for God given doctors and medicine? Luke was Paul's travelling companion and was now with him in Rome. Paul calls him 'beloved', or 'dear', and so he must have been as Paul suffered from the frequent illness that never left him (Galatians 4:13, 2 Cor 10:10). There is no doubt that Luke would have ministered to Paul's needs and through his God given medical abilities, brought relief to the great Apostle.

So too, in our day and age, we can thank God for His direct intervention in divine healing, but also pray for and rejoice in those who serve in the healing professions. And so, Luke sends his greetings along with Demas. Whilst Luke inspires us, Demas warns us. Here he is included among those with Paul and is in fellowship with the brethren. However, the way of the world is a snare that entices and traps, and so it would be with Demas. Later he would abandon Paul and return to the way of the world (2 Timothy 4:10). So, the believers must guard their hearts so that they may not stumble and lose their crown of victory.

*Colossians 4:15*

*"Greet the brethren who are in Laodicea and also Nympha and the church that is in [her] house."*

Paul sends greetings to the brethren in Laodicea who were the local church. The identity of this person, Nympha, is unknown and manuscripts vary in the rendering of the pronoun, offering 'her', 'him' and 'theirs' in relation to the name. It is most certainly a shortening of the name Nymphodorus. Paul uses 'his house', giving weight to the person being a man.

The suggestion is that Paul is greeting Nympha as one of 'the brethren' who make up the local church that meet in their, i.e. Nymphodorus's house. What is notable here is that the early Church did not have large buildings to meet in but fellowshipped in local homes. Paul would encourage the opening of homes, even to strangers (Rom 12:13), as did the writer to the Hebrews (Heb 13:2). Truly reflective of Jesus are open homes and open hearts.

*Colossians 4:16*

*"When this letter is read among you, have it also read in the church of the Laodiceans; and you, for your part read my letter that is coming from Laodicea."*

The letters from Paul were a valuable source of spiritual development for the early Gentile Christians, as teaching from their Apostle. Remember there was no codified 'book' as we have today. Writing letters in Paul's time and having them delivered was no easy matter. In our modern day of easy postal services, we can forget this fact. Hence Paul instructs the precious document to be read to the nearby Laodicean church.

I am reminded of the church in China, who starved of Christian literature, treated every Christian letter and document with great respect. Every document was taken and shared among Christian groups over areas of hundreds of miles. I had two friends who took Bibles into China, when they were banned. They often spoke of the great joy and celebration when a Bible reached a village.

So, it was in the early Church, before the canon of the book of the Early Church Texts was fixed in the fourth century, that letters like Colossians was a very precious document.

The reference to the letter coming from Laodicea is to a letter that no longer exists. Many think it to be the letter we know as Ephesians, but there is no real basis for this. A Latin forgery did emerge in the early Church, but it has been rightly dismissed as a hotchpotch of Scripture, mainly Philippians.

> **Colossians 4:17**
> **"Say to Archippus, "Take heed to the ministry which you have received in the Lord, that you may fulfil it."**

Archippus is here mentioned. In the letter which accompanied this one to Philemon, he is described as Paul's fellow soldier (Philm 1:2). He is also a member of Philemon's household and might even have been his son (*ibid*). The soldier of the Lord has much battling and the war can take its toll. Archippus, according to the language, had a calling in the Lord to ministry. Whatever that ministry was, Archippus needed encouragement. It is unclear whether Paul's words are a rebuke or a simple reminder to Archippus, not to give up.

Whichever it was, Paul is encouraging all the Colossian hearers to deliver his message. They are to 'say to Archippus'. It is a spiritually mature fellowship and mature leadership that can make room for the community to speak to ministers. It is the responsibility of all members to speak into the lives of their ministers, with grace and love. Never to harm or hurt, but to encourage the soldiers of the Lord to continue the good fight. It is the whole body working as one, so that all can fulfil their ministries and to advance the Kingdom of the Cosmic Christ.

*Colossians 4:18*

*"I, Paul, writing this greeting with my own hand. Remember my bonds. Grace be with you."*

And so, Paul, having dictated the letter to a scribe, takes the parchment. And with his hand chained to a Roman soldier, takes the writing implement, and authenticates the letter with his final salutation. This was common practice for the Apostle to speak the words and for a fellow worker to write them down to be sent to the churches (See 1 Cor. And 2 Thess). But so that the community might know that the words had his Apostolic authority, Paul writes the closing sentence.

He ends the letter by asking the Colossians to remember his bonds as is the Greek or imprisonment, as some translate. Paul's imprisonment was the confirmation of his struggle to bring the Gospel to the Gentiles. How right and fitting that those who were blessed by Paul's ministry should remember him in their thoughts and prayers. Every community of believers need to heed these words and to frequently call to mind those who struggle in torture and imprisonment even today, for the sake of the Gospel. The prayers of the saints are spiritual power to such brothers and sisters.

The final thought of Paul is that the grace of God would be with them. This is the fifth time in this letter Paul has made mention of grace. It is through grace that God has reached down to save men from sin. It is in grace the child of God lives. It is a facet of the inheritance of the saints. The heretics of Colossae had tried to disturb the believers, to move them from faithful living in the grace of the Cosmic Christ. Paul, inspired of the Spirit, makes sure the last thought they are left with, is one of grace.

AMEN!

# Scripture Index

## The Tanach Texts

## The Early Church Texts

15:22 .............................. 96
15:32 .............................. 66
15:42 .............................. 62
15:42-58 .......................... 89
15:48-49 .......................... 138
16:9 .............................. 165

2 Corinthians
3:18 .............................. 85
4:4 .............................. 37
4:10-14 .......................... 89
5:6-8 .............................. 89
5:16 .............................. 35
5:21 .............................. 86, 94
10:5 .............................. 81
10:10 .............................. 175
11:13-15 .......................... 74
11:22-33 .......................... 6
11:23-28 .......................... 52
11:33 .............................. 165
12:1-12 .......................... 6

Galatians
1:11-12 .......................... 6
2:2 .............................. 56
2:20 .............................. 124
3:28 .............................. 59, 139
4:3 .............................. 82
4:4 .............................. 105
4:13 .............................. 175
5:6 .............................. 11
5:24 .............................. 88
6:15 .............................. 139

Ephesians
1:7 .............................. 33, 61
1:7-12 .......................... 151
1:18 .............................. 61
1:20-23 .......................... 37

1:22-23 .............................. 44
2 .............................. 123
2:1-2 .............................. 131
2:3-7 .............................. 96
2:7 .............................. 61
2:8 .............................. 9
2:8-9 .............................. 158
2:10 .............................. 24, 123
2:11-15 .............................. 140
2:12 .............................. 60
2:14-17 .............................. 139
2:15 .............................. 7, 101
2:22 .............................. 46
3:1-12 .............................. 58
3:2 .............................. 7
3:7-8 .............................. 7
3:9-1 .............................. 71
3:9-10 .............................. 55
3:10 .............................. 32
3:17 .............................. 77
4:13 .............................. 64
4:16 .............................. 68
4:24 .............................. 136
4:25 .............................. 135
5 .............................. 154
5:6 .............................. 129
5:22 .............................. 153
5:27 .............................. 86
6:4 .............................. 9
6:7 .............................. 157
6:20 .............................. 9

Philippians
1:3 .............................. 10
1:4 .............................. 10
1:6 .............................. 50
1:9 .............................. 165

Printed in Great Britain
by Amazon

33323621R00106